zabeth Islands

GREENLAND

Baffin Bay

Davis Strait

Baffin Island

Foxe
Basin

ge Bay

Hudson Strait

Labrador Sea

Hudson Bay

Halifax

Arctic Circle

MOUNTIE IN MUKLUKS

MOUNTIE IN MUKLUKS

The Arctic Adventures of Bill White

Patrick White

with a foreword by Edith Iglauer

HARBOUR PUBLISHING

Harbour Publishing Co. Ltd.
P.O. Box 219
Madeira Park, BC
V0N 2H0
www.harbourpublishing.com

THE CANADA COUNCIL | LE CONSEIL DES ARTS
FOR THE ARTS | DU CANADA
SINCE 1957 | DEPUIS 1957

Cover design by Peter Read
Printed and bound in Canada

BRITISH
COLUMBIA
ARTS COUNCIL
Supported by the Province of British Columbia

Harbour Publishing acknowledges financial support from the Government of Canada through the Book Publishing Industry Development Program and the Canada Council for the Arts, and from the Province of British Columbia through the British Columbia Arts Council and the Book Publisher's Tax Credit through the Ministry of Provincial Revenue.

Library and Archives Canada Cataloguing in Publication

White, Patrick, 1981–
    Mountie in mukluks : the Arctic adventures of Bill White / Patrick White.

ISBN 1-55017-352-9

    1. White, Bill, 1905–2001. 2. Cambridge Bay Region (Nunavut)—History. 3. Inuit—Social life and customs. 4. Canada, Northern—History. 5. Royal Canadian Mounted Police—Biography. 6. Cambridge Bay Region (Nunavut)—Biography. 7. Canada, Northern—Biography. I. Title.

FC3216.3.W47W47 2004   971.9'502'092   C2004-904081-2

CONTENTS

FOREWORD

I wish that I had had this amazing account of Bill White's experiences in the North to read before I went to the Canadian Arctic myself. This slim volume was exactly what I needed to give me background in preparation for the trips I took north on assignment for *The New Yorker* magazine beginning in 1961, which eventually became the basis for my books *Inuit Journey* and *Denison's Ice Road*. His book makes fascinating reading now. In graphic detail and outrageous language Bill gives the real story of what people and conditions were like in the Canadian Arctic seventy years ago. Relating his personal experiences with total candor, he takes us right into the Inuit communities and his close relationships with individual Inuk, and into the official and unofficial lives of the police officers stationed in their midst. We are there when he is sizing up the oddball characters who still drift in and out of far northern communities. In fact, we are with Bill all the way with his rare and valuable view of Canada's north when it was feeling the first effects of exploration and the southern hunger for natural resources—a transformation that has changed that land forever, not necessarily for the better.

When William Shawn, my editor at *The New Yorker*, first sent me into the Far North to report on the development of Inuit co-operatives, to ride the ice road and later to accompany Prime Minister Pierre Trudeau, I could find nothing reliable to read about conditions in the modern Arctic. I was an innocent, a wide-eyed American journalist from a conventional middle-class family, without experience or any knowledge of where exactly I was going. James Houston, a writer friend with long north-ern experience, recommended some historical reading material, but there was nothing like *Mountie in Mukluks* available in 1961. When I got there I went into shock. This new Arctic was so raw but so exhilarating; so harsh but so beautiful; so troubled, with no economic or social solutions in sight, but so engaging. My first northern encounter was such a surprise that when I came back to New York I told my younger son Richard I felt as if I was returning from Mars. Reading Bill White's spare but colourful descriptions of the harsh realities, I am on familiar ground.

What Patrick White (no relation) has woven together is a marvellous account, in Bill's own words, of how he became an RCMP officer and started as a seaman on the famous RCMP Arctic patrol ship, the *St. Roch*, then went on shore posting in Cambridge Bay, an Inuit settlement in the Central Arctic. The only reason he joined the force in the first place, he said, was to explore the North, do some trapping and get to know the Inuit. And know them he did! He appreciated aboriginal values and the magic of their stark landscape. Life for the Inuit still revolved almost entirely around the eternal quest for food and shelter, and Bill, a cynic by nature and experience, was awed by the philosophical but practical sensibilities at the base of their survival over thousands of years.

His untamed chronicles are bawdy, brave, sometimes cruel, sometimes hilarious—and always truthful. He had a compulsion to tell the truth, which he laced with his special wild humour, no matter where it led him. We are lucky in this legacy. In his tapes he said he was telling it the way it was, and he did. One of the more benign passages in the book is Bill's description of the only depth sounder the *St. Roch* possessed as it moved through treacherous ice-bound waters, which gave me goose pimples as I read it. It was, he said, ". . . an eight-pound hunk of round lead with a dimple in the bottom and a jeezly long piece of rope tied to it that you . . . swung . . . around a few times and then tossed a good fifteen feet ahead of the boat so that it'd be sitting on the bottom by the time the boat caught up with it." The only thing that stopped the *Roch* from going up on the rocks was the guy on the lead, he continued. "You'd get so doggone tired you'd feel like you were lifting a cannonball out of the water. And the water up there, oh she's cold. There'd be a roostertail coming off that line as you pulled it in and it'd piss all over you. After an hour or so, your hands wouldn't move. The skin on them would be cracked from all the salt and chafing. You couldn't take that for more than an hour at a time, so you went out there in short shifts."

Some years later I met Bill White and his gentle, lovely wife Ivy shortly after I came to live in Pender Harbour, at a housewarming. He was a big man with a full red face and large eyeglasses behind which watchful eyes took in the whole available landscape. In his later years, when I saw him frequently, he clumped around, his big heavy body bent from arthritis. He leaned on a cane, but he radiated energy and purpose. He was always busy, gardening on his rocky bluff when he wasn't fulminating against authority. He made handsome tabletops and clocks set into beautiful burnished wood from the burls that he found in the surrounding forests. He was generous with his approval, ferocious in his disdain for cheaters and hypocrites, and full of fun, with a pointed wit that made him a pleasure to be with.

At our first meeting, we immediately began comparing Arctic experiences, a subject on which we both were hooked. He had read about the birth of Inuit co-operatives in *Inuit Journey* and he eagerly questioned me. Satisfied that I knew the difference between the fictional Eskimo and authentic Inuit, he launched into a battery of fascinating remarks about the *St. Roch* and its master, Henry Larsen, all the while rejoicing in his own tenure on this historic vessel that now rests on dry land at the Maritime Museum in Vancouver. Our conversations continued intermittently for the rest of his life.

After his wife passed away Bill was lost, and talking with friends became his only real pleasure. An invitation to dinner was instantly accepted and despite a firmly set time of six o'clock he would arrive two or three hours early, engaging his hosts in such animated talk that cooking was a hazard. Along about five he would often show up around the stove, lifting lids and peering in suspiciously to see what was taking so long. Having Bill to dinner involved most of the day, and a wise host learned to prepare in advance. I suspect his brusque manner covered an innate shyness with people for whom he had real affection, but it was a force to contend with nevertheless. He was one tough guy.

Writing oral history is not easy to do well and Patrick White, working from live interviews, archive papers and a mass of audio tapes randomly accumulated over the decades, has served his subject brilliantly. The purple language in the book is vintage Bill, especially the lacerating remarks about notable northerners like Henry Larsen, the *St. Roch's* celebrated skipper, for whom he also had grudging affection, or the RCMP officials he brushed against during his service. No one escaped his scathing tongue, especially phonies, whom he could spot a mile off. His unique expressions, his humorous asides, even the narrations of northern drinking sprees that would have killed ordinary humans, have been retained in this wonderful portrait of a unique Canadian.

—EDITH IGLAUER

INTRODUCTION

Even without reading this book, people the world over would recognize the main features of RCMP Constable Bill White's Arctic experiences, although they might be surprised by his unusual take on them. The myth of the dog-sledding Mountie who always gets his man is a tip of the stiff-brimmed Stetson in Bill's direction. In the early 1930s he was stationed in Cambridge Bay, a tiny outpost nestled between tundra and ice floes about 1,850 kilometres as the ptarmigan flies northeast of Edmonton, Alberta. One of the things he did while serving there was to complete an eighteen-hundred-kilometre dogsled trip that resulted in a murder conviction. The attendant media ballyhoo spread across the continent, and whether it influenced MGM's decision to remake the iconic Mountie film *Rose Marie* the following year is a matter for speculation. Certainly Bill's good press added materially to the myth of RCMP invincibility in the North.

What sets Bill's story apart is that he so vigorously rejects that myth and devotes such energy to exploding it in the pages that follow. He was a born iconoclast who resigned from the force upon leaving the Arctic and became a noted labour activist. As an Arctic redcoat he was decidedly *not* with the program and essentially went native, immersing himself in Inuit culture and taking the Inuit side against his non-Native colleagues at every opportunity.

Bill White's story touches on another Arctic legend as he recounts his two stints as crewman on the RCMP patrol ship *St. Roch* under Captain Henry Larsen. The *St. Roch* was later placed on permanent display at the Vancouver Maritime Museum and Henry Larsen became one of Canada's enduring Arctic heroes, with an Arctic body of water and a modern 10,000-horsepower Coast Guard icebreaker named in his honour. Bill liked Larsen personally but was bemused by the unassuming seaman's elevation to heroic stature.

Six of the Mounties Bill worked with in the Arctic eventually wrote books about their experiences. Like most of the books he read on the Arctic, they infuriated him. They trumpeted the heroics of the force and made the Inuit look foolish, a reverse of the truth as Bill knew it. His disdain for the common run of northern Mounties who never learned how to build an igloo or speak Inuktitut was exceeded only by his affection and admiration for the Inuit, which became a lifelong passion. For years Bill dreamed of writing a book of his own that would tell it "the way it was"—his working title. At one point he sat down and taped the whole story by himself, but without a live audience the spark went out of his storytelling and the resulting 170-page transcript read like an overlong police report.

In the early 1970s he approached my father, Howard White, who was a neighbour (there is no family connection) and was just embarking on a writing career. They began taping, but soon got sidetracked by Bill's other life as a labour leader. They produced a book alright, but *A Hard Man to Beat* (1983) is a rollicking account of Bill's decade at the helm of the Marine Workers Union and contains scarcely a mention of the North.

They always intended to get back to the original project and Dad talked to Bill hundreds of times over the next twenty-five years, making hours of tape, but to Bill's frustration it never went beyond that. As he often pointed out, not one of those six Mounties who wrote books about sailing on the *St. Roch* lived to see their manuscript published, and he wanted to one-up his old adversaries by attending his own book launch. Alas, fate had other plans. Bill White's long campaign to set the record straight and come out on top of a seventy-year rivalry ended at age ninety-six in a Ladner, BC, nursing home on July 20, 2001.

Bill White recalling a story in the living room of his Pender Harbour home, 1990.

I knew little about his unfinished project until 2000 when I found a couple of the old tapes in my dad's office and plugged them into my stereo. Their vitality and freshness astonished me. I had known a very different Bill when I was a child. To me he was a scary old guy with a cane who had an uncanny ability to time his daily phone calls for the exact moment our family was sitting down to supper, proceeding to hold forth on the day's news headlines while the vegetables went cold. Whenever I saw him in person he'd demand to know if I was the one stealing apples off his tree, then peer into my eyes for any trace of deception in my answer.

The first time I heard these recordings, about a year before he died, I realized there was more than I imagined behind those beady old eyes. As a history student I saw a valuable primary resource documenting the early days of our country's formal intervention in the Arctic, and as a sucker for a good story I saw an opportunity for a great book. But I was just starting my university education and couldn't do anything about it, so the material continued to sit in the drawer while the clock ran out on Bill's long vigil.

A couple of weeks after Bill White passed away, his daughter Marilyn Bueckert fulfilled one of his last requests by sending my dad a forty-ounce bottle of Crown Royal. Everybody understood this was a very special bottle that could only be tapped for a very special purpose, so it sat unopened. Then one hot August night a spectacular meteor shower animated the sky. Just as we stepped outside to watch the show, Dad surprised me by taking out Bill's bottle of rye. Under a sky lit up by shooting stars, he broke the seal, took a sip and passed it to me. "I think Bill would approve," he said. But no sooner had he spoken than the bottle slipped from his grip and smashed on the pavement. Dad felt awful, but there was something very portentous about the moment that we both felt. I'm convinced it was Bill's way of saying, "Quit screwing around and finish my damn book."

Here you go, Bill. Sorry it took so long.

—PATRICK WHITE

A Note on the Writing

Bill was a master raconteur but he assumed his listeners knew far more background about things like the *Baymaud* and the *Bay Chimo* than most of us do today. I combed his quarter-century of recordings for bits of explanatory context and pasted them in where needed. I took specific questions to my grandfather, Frank White, and my dad, who were often able to recall details from their years of listening to Bill chew the fat. Names and dates I cross-referenced as well as I could from other books, archive documents and web pages, and I took the liberty of correcting Bill's memory when it was clearly off, which was not often. Bill's ability to remember Inuit names and words after seven decades was uncanny but it was seldom possible to verify spellings. My apologies to the families of these pioneers for the inevitable errors. During the long gestation of this book the term "Eskimo" was replaced in common usage by "Inuit" and, as Bill started with one and ended with the other, I have taken the liberty of standardizing all occurrences to "Inuit." Other than that, any passages that might be considered vulgar or politically incorrect by our standards I have tried my best to retain. Oral history, as my father wrote in his introduction to *A Hard Man to Beat*, should strive to "capture the real world through the real language of a real person."

1

RECRUITING A CRIMINAL

I never wanted to be a cop. Christ, I didn't want to spend my life handing out traffic tickets. I joined the RCMP so I could get up north. There was nothing more to it. It was funny how it happened—I had to get on the wrong side of the law first.

It was the spring of '28 and I'd spent three months trapping muskrat six or seven miles north of the homestead. It was rough country that time of year, but there was a hell of a bumper crop of rats. I ended up trapping five or six hundred at a buck and a half each. That was when the average joe was pulling in three bucks a day. Not a lot of people knew the rats were there, and I wasn't about to let anybody in on the secret.

I was pretty damn smug until this bastard Weimer started stealing from my traps. I knew because the stupid bugger left his tracks all around. Boy, did I want to fix that son of a bitch. I saw him coming up the trail towards me one morning along my line, so I crouched down behind a bush and popped off a couple warning shots. I wasn't trying to hit him; I just wanted to blow a little mud up around his feet. He thought sure as shit that I was trying to kill him, and runs off and tells the cops. They had a big Jesus investigation—brought an inspector up from Weyburn and everything. When they asked I said, "Christ, the old guy's nuts. I'd never shoot at him." They asked me if I had done any shooting while I was out trapping. I told them, "Yes, I was shooting rabbit, but I never seen the old bugger." I guess Weimer had a bit of a reputation because I got off without putting up much of a fight.

A week later I met this Weimer up in the hills again and I just beat the shit out of the old bastard. He was no pushover, probably forty years old and a big build on him, but I managed to work him over pretty good. I figured a good bruising would fix him and I wouldn't have to worry about him again. But no, he went straight to the cops again, this time claiming I'd assaulted him. This cop by the name of Usher came out from Ogema, a little place about ten miles southwest of us. He charged me with assault and hauled me into town. They had two magistrates there. One was a no-good bastard who didn't like me. I'd had a few run-ins with him and I knew he'd find me guilty, so I got up and objected to him sitting on the trial. I said he was prejudiced against me. For some reason that argument held water and the judge was taken off the case. I figured I had a better chance with this other magistrate—he didn't know me. Neither of us had lawyers. I argued that Weimer had come after me and I was forced to defend myself. I got off again.

That Usher saw right through my bullshit. After the trial he come up to me and said, "Look, you're gonna end up dead or in jail if you keep on this way. If you want to trap, get on with the Mounties and head up north. You can do all the trapping you want up there and get paid for it." He figured me and Weimer were headed for another big rhubarb.

I'd read about the North. She was bloody primitive then. The RCMP couldn't detail you to the Arctic in those days. You had to volunteer, and because of that they were always hard up for constables up north. Most of those cops didn't want any hardships. They'd rather ride around in a car and have a meal in a café. So I decided to join with an eye on getting to the Arctic as soon as possible. I suppose that was a relief to everyone around Amulet, Saskatchewan.

2

PRAIRIE BOY

Most people think of the Arctic as some awful, inhospitable place, but it really isn't much different than the Prairies. We had nearly everything that makes the Arctic hard to live in: cold, wind, ice and lunatics.

I was born around the Muskoka Lakes in Ontario in 1905, and we moved out to a one-room shack in Yellow Grass, Saskatchewan, when I was three.[1] We lived in that thing from the winter of '08 to '09 and the snow sometimes came right through the cracks in the walls, she was so poorly built. Dad delivered water around town all winter. Had to haul it several miles with a bobsled and a team of horses and sold it for five cents a pail.

We weren't long in Yellow Grass. As soon as spring came around, Dad hitched up the horses and took us off to a homestead he'd filed the year before about five miles northwest of Amulet.[2]

---

1. Lundy William Lloyd White was born 1905 and died July 20, 2001, in Vancouver, aged 96.
2. Amulet, Saskatchewan was not officially named until 1910, when work began to build a rail line through the town. A railway official gave the town its name when he discovered an amulet on the town's temporary train platform.

That place was hell and gone away from everything—twenty-five miles to the nearest railroad station in Forward. It was a good two-day trip to go there and back with horses, which seems a hardship now, but we thought nothing of it.

Dad built a shack at the homestead before he brought the rest of the family out. He called it a house, but I think it measured about twelve feet by twenty feet. First thing he did after getting this shack up was plow a fireguard around it and burn off all the prairie grass. I can still remember coming over a rise in the trail leading to the shack—there were no roads at the time—and Dad saying, "There it is." Jesus, it was just as plain as could be. We'd been expecting a house and here was this shack surrounded by burned-off grass and old buffalo bones. I don't think my mother was too impressed. I already had one brother and there was another on the way. It was crowded alright.

Compared to others in the area, that shack wasn't so bad. Ours had a wood frame, and that was when lumber was bloody expensive. Most houses around there were made of sod. Sod actually made for better insulation. We used to bank it up all around the base of our shack. In the wintertime we'd build snow blocks and stack them on top of the sod all the way up the sides

The twelve- by twenty-foot home where Bill's parents raised four sons.

of the house, just like you do in the North. Then Dad would throw water on it and it'd freeze on the outside so the wind wouldn't cut it away.

It was a good goddamn thing Dad kept those fireguards up. Must've been 1910 when we had the big prairie fire. Dad was out there day and night plowing extra fireguards. And the sky, it was full of smoke getting thicker and thicker. It got to be where you couldn't see for more than twenty feet or so. I remember Dad saying, "It'll soon be here." He was right. There was this wall of flame travelling about as fast as a man can run. We had a small lake in front of us. That, along with the guards, saved us. I'll never forget that place after the fire went through. You felt like you were in a different world. All that brown grass was completely burnt. Everything was black.

Growing up in that country was better preparation for the Arctic than anything I learned in basic training. Every year you'd get a few blizzards so bad, people would get lost. Dad used to stretch binder twine between the house and the barn so he wouldn't get turned around in a blizzard and lose sight of the house. There were a lot of lives lost like that. One time in the winter our neighbour, a fellow by the name of Tom Whittle, came over for supper. He brought a little lamp with him because it was getting dark early by that time of year. He stuck around and talked with Dad for a while and then headed for home in a straight-on blizzard. About half an hour later we saw a light coming back down the hill. We waited for a bit and along came Tom. When he saw Dad open the door, old Tom started swearing to beat hell. He got turned around in the blizzard and walked toward the light in our house thinking it was his own. I believe he made it home on the second try.

Dad trained us up quick in the different ways you could catch animals. When we first got there he gave us kids some little gopher traps. When we got a little bigger we trapped badgers, muskrats and weasels. Badgers actually fetched a pretty good price then. They used the hair for top-of-the-line hair brushes. I was always keen on trapping and I was pretty good at it. There's a real trick to how you set those traps. You have to make kind of a shell out of snow to fit over top of the trap. You shape this snow so it's concave on the bottom, to fit over the trap, and flat on top. When you put this thin shell of snow over top of the trap you throw a few flakes of dried fish or something on top, just enough to attract the critter you're after. The shell collapses and the trap slams shut as soon as anything gets close to the bait

There was always fishing going on. One winter, just after I was out of high school, I commercial fished up in Doré Lake. That's getting into northern country. We fished just like they did in the Arctic. I think we had twenty-seven miles of nets strung under the ice. We wore deerskin clothing and got around with dogs. The only thing we didn't have was igloos, but we could've, she was colder than a witch's tit up there.

Another thing you had to get used to in the Arctic was damn strange characters—not the Inuit so much, usually it was the whites who were a little nuts—and there was ample training for that in Saskatchewan as well. I'd met my share of queer buggers by the time I was ten. One of the strangest had to be R.F. Taylor, an Aussie who came up to Amulet to teach at the little school-house we had there. He always wore a Mounted Police coat and a big Stetson hat. He only had one leg and claimed to've lost the other in the Boer War. There'd been a lot of horse-rustling going on around Amulet at the time, so Taylor told Dad and a few others that he was really an undercover cop sent to round up the rustlers. He had the six-shooter to prove it. I know that much because he used to keep it on his desk at the schoolhouse. Every now and then he'd pick it up and point it down at us kids. We'd just freeze. Then the old bastard would saunter to a window at the back of the room and empty six shots into a tree.

Taylor stayed at our house for quite some time. That's just how it was then—if a guy didn't have a house, you always offered him a bed. One time he went out with my parents to a school concert and returned without them. He was complaining of stomach pains, so we put him in bed. He was right off his rocker, sweating and screaming about the pain. After a while my folks got back to the house and Dad went into town to get a doctor. The doctor couldn't come right away, but he said that it sounded like Taylor had appendicitis. He came out the next day with another doctor from Weyburn. They operated on the old bastard right on the kitchen table. I remember that so goddamn well. They had a hell of a time putting him under, exhausted about half a dozen bottles of ether before they finally knocked him out. I guess that's when they started getting a little suspicious.

The doctor from Weyburn was something of a specialist. He put a split right down Taylor's belly, and I remember thinking it looked just like bacon. Then they started pulling his guts out and got a big bunch of it out before yarding out his appendix. The specialist looked at it for a while and said, "Well, that's not his trouble." They had to slide the guts back in without operating. Then they sewed him up and put him back to bed. The local doctor left a dozen morphine tablets for the pain. He put the tablets in the top drawer of the dresser and told Mom to use them only if absolutely necessary. When the doctor came back about four days later, he asked if we had to use any of the tablets. Mom said no and went to the dresser to give these pills back to the doctor, but they were gone. The doctor told her then that he figured Taylor was a hop-head. He told this whole story just to get his hands on some dope. He was supposed to be a veteran and a cop, but we soon learned that that was all bullshit. Imagine having your belly split open just to get your hands on some pills.

We kept him around long enough to get better. He started borrowing an old horse at night and riding off, pretending to chase rustlers. He told us that he met them one night and exchanged a few shots, but they managed to get away. A couple days later he disappeared. The police showed up at the schoolhouse to take his hat and coat. We never heard from him again.

I never did like going to school. I had to trudge six or seven miles to the schoolhouse through all kinds of weather and then learn things I never did find any use for. But I finished high school with decent enough grades, so after that spell up at Doré Lake I went down to college in Regina.

Higher learning didn't much appeal to me either. I was more interested in sports. I played ball all the time. I was a pretty fair pitcher too—once struck out nineteen batters in one game. I belonged to boxing and wrestling clubs as well, but managed to pass my first year of college all the same. One year was enough. I was qualified to teach but never really had any desire for it.

Then I started booming around, working on farms all over the continent. That was one hell of a life. You'd just show up for harvests all over. You could be in Kansas one week and Manitoba the next and Montana after that. The only real trick to it was outrunning the goddamn border patrol, but I got pretty good at slipping through in places I knew they didn't watch.

You don't get up to much good in a life like that. I usually had all sorts of travelling partners—some of them good fellas, some of them rotten crooks. We'd work at these farms cutting hay or what have you, and then get paid in a big lump sum. That always meant we'd go on a big drunk in the nearest town, maybe get into a rhubarb and then skip town.

At twenty-four, I went back home for the winter one last time. I remember coming into town that year and seeing crosses burning. The Ku Klux Klan[3] was becoming a big presence up there. Everyone was joining the bloody Klan. They were all Anglicans around there and most of them joined just because it was anti-Catholic and anti-Liberal. I remember them burning crosses all over the place, and not knowing what to make of it. That was the year I joined the Mounties.

---

3. The Ku Klux Klan entered Saskatchewan in 1926. Two years later the group claimed to have a membership of 70,000 in the province, mainly on the strength of its anti-Catholic, anti-Liberal propaganda. It launched a major campaign against separate schools in 1928, calling for "one public school" that would not teach religion or French. Though never formally associated with the opposition Conservatives, both groups aimed to unseat the Liberals and advocate for non-sectarian schools.

3

BASIC TRAINING

I had a close partner in crime in Amulet and managed to convince him to join the Mounties with me. We figured the force would offer more adventure than knocking around rural Saskatchewan. We both headed off to Weyburn for the recruitment tests. In those days the whole process only took a day or so. You had to do a written test to make sure you knew the difference between right and wrong, and a physical. I managed to pretty well bullshit my way through all that, but my friend never did lie as well as I did. He headed back to Amulet and I headed north to Regina for basic training.[4]

The regime they put us through in Regina was pretty much all bullshit. Mainly we were lectured on shooting, riding and the Criminal Code. Well shit, I'd been raised on a bloody horse and I'd been handling guns from a young age. Not more than a year prior I'd competed in provincial shooting matches and won quite a wad, so I could shoot as well or better than anyone there. Their idea of horsemanship was the old cavalry style. They had

---

4. Regina's "depot" division has been the national training centre for the Royal Canadian Mounted Police.

Bill was an experienced horseman when he joined the Mounties, but not in the RCMP's old cavalry style of riding.

these little postage-stamp saddles, and you had to bounce up and down to demonstrate you were a distinguished *rouge*. I was a good rider, but I couldn't ride for them bastards. I don't know what the point of most of their bullshit was. It was really nothing more than a modified Boy Scouts program. You could spend days learning how to peg a bloody tent.

And they always kept you busy with pointless little manoeuvres. Before breakfast they lined you up out by the stables for inspection, then you had to groom the horses. After breakfast it was drills—march, right turn, left turn, present arms and all that bullshit.

The best part of basic training was learning the Criminal Code. There's a lot of goddamn strange things you wouldn't expect in the Criminal Code. For instance, it said that it was against the law to try and screw a dame on a boat. Us recruits got more laughs out of that book than any other kind of smut we managed to smuggle in there.

There was a lot of miserable old bastards kicking around there. One of the worst was Jocky Jones. He ran the cavalry regiment, and sometimes he'd come out early in the morning and go through the ride with us. They had one horse there by the name of Jigs and he was pretty snorty. You really had to watch that horse. Jocky went out one morning and got behind another rider who was on Jigs. Jigs bucked and old Jocky just flew right out of the saddle. Jocky didn't even see it coming. We saw him lying way down a hill. He must've rolled a good hundred feet. Buns King—he was one of the guys the Mad Trapper shot—and I ran down to Jocky. We got ahold of him, but he had one bum leg that wouldn't work, and he was so goddamn drunk there was no way he'd keep his balance on the good one. He just absolutely reeked of booze. I'm not sure how he managed to mount a horse in that condition. We packed him up to a truck and drove him to the hospital.

After a few weeks Jocky came back with a bit of a limp. Never even bothered to thank Buns and I. A couple days went by and one morning Jocky put on a pair of real sharp spurs. A few of us were watching this and we knew damn well what he was up to. He went and mounted Jigs and rode that horse till the blood was running down its side. I never seen a horse played out like poor old Jigs. He just lay there with his legs spread out and head hanging down. Jocky got off and kicked the horse in the belly, but it wouldn't budge.

Part of every recruit's duty was to fend off the reds. There was a communist scare even then, and the RCMP figured communists were going to pop out of the bushes and burn down the stables, so there had to be a guard out there at all times. You'd do guard duty at night, and you had to go through all six of the big stables. There was a Sergeant Akins who made damn sure you did a thorough search. Every night he poked around outside with a flashlight making sure the guard was doing his job. He thought he was pretty stealthy about it, but you always knew Flashlight Akins was watching you. Everybody hated him because the minute you sat down or went to the bushes for a piss, Flashlight Akins would flip his beam on and tear a strip off you for dereliction of duty or some stupid thing.

One night Akins really got what was coming to him. This one recruit, a real tough bugger, was on night watch and he knew old Akins was following him. So he went into one of the stables through the back door and shut it behind him. Then he just stood beside the door and waited. So Akins comes along and slowly slides the door open just like he's a cat burglar, and this guy just clobbers him, knocks him flat on the ground. They didn't discipline him or nothing. He said he mistook Akins for a commie.

Another shitheel was Sergeant Pete Irvine. We called him Diarrhea Pete. We had to take revolver practice with him. Irvine spent most of the class bragging about how good a shot he was. There was one old fella in the class, Sam, who was just back for refresher training. Sam was a real good shot—won the Canadian championship a few years before I met him. I bought a gun they presented to him at the championship. The old bugger was always broke, and he sold me that gun for twenty-five bucks. This Diarrhea Pete figured he could beat Sam no problem, and mouthed off about it steady. One day Pete decided he was going to really show how good a shot he was. He walked up to the shooting gallery early in the morning and came back down at breakfast to hand Sam a paper target that had a perfect circle of bullet holes around the bull's eye. Pete said, "I betchya never seen someone do that before."

Well, Diarrhea Pete tried to bullshit the wrong group of guys. Sitting with us was a farrier who'd seen Pete that morning up at the shooting range standing five feet away from this target, filling it full of holes. You were supposed to stand sixty yards away. Diarrhea Pete got all red in the face and tried to defend himself. "How could you even think I would do such a thing?" he said. He really tried to give the farrier hell, but we all knew Pete was fulla shit. That's why we called him Diarrhea Pete.

After a few months of this bullshit, they sent ten of us out for some real work. That was when the Sons of Freedom sect of the Doukhobors were raising quite a ruckus in the Kamsack–Veregin area, just north of Regina.[5] There were three sects of Doukhobor: the independent Doukhobor, who was the same as anyone else; the community Doukhobor, who was real socialist; and the Sons of Freedom, they were the real radical ones. The Freedomites didn't believe in sending their kids to school and had burned around thirty schoolhouses. Our job was to patrol the area on horseback just to make sure no more schools went up. I think it was one of the last times the RCMP patrolled with horses.

---

5. The Doukhobors were a sect of Russian Christians that arose in the 18th century. Persecution at home brought around 7,500 to Saskatchewan and Manitoba in 1899, where the Canadian government granted them land and promised tolerance in the practice of their beliefs. The government eventually reneged on the promise, taking back land, requiring an oath to the British Crown and making school attendance mandatory for children. The dissident Sons of Freedom sect of the Doukhobors fought back with arson, bombs and nude marches.

A few of these Freedomites were caught in the act one day so we hauled a couple guys into the Kamsack station. Well, the shit really hit the fan then. About three hundred of them started marching from Veregin to Kamsack to protest the arrests. On the way they peeled off all their clothes. We rushed out to stop them at the bridge just before town. It was quite a revelation to us young recruits, who had never seen a naked woman in broad daylight before. And this was no beauty pageant. Later on when the Freedomites started making news in BC, their leader was a woman known as Big Fanny. I don't know if a big fanny is an asset for a Doukhobor leader, but if so there was a lot of talent on view that day at the Kamsack bridge. They issued itching powder to all us guys on horseback and we went around throwing this stuff on the poor old girls. It wasn't one of the RCMP's proudest moments.

We managed to stop them on the bridge, but none of them wanted to put their clothes back on, so we had to arrest them. This presented a bit of a logistics problem. We had to press six or seven local grain trucks into service to corral them all. They were all big girls, most had me by forty pounds or more, and they had mastered the art of passive resistance. I made damn sure I was in the truck pulling up rather than boosting from below. Once

Doukhobors marching toward the bridge into Kamsack before they shed their clothes.

Mounties waiting with a group of arrested marchers for grain trucks to come and take them away.

we loaded them, we just threw their clothes in the trucks and off they went. They had a mass trial and most of them got six months in the Prince Albert Penitentiary.

I felt bad for those Freedomites. One old girl came up to me during that nude parade and showed me her bare ass. There was a good-sized imprint of a boot sole that was all black and blue. One of the cops must have done that. It was just bloody cruel.

They gave us a couple days break from patrolling now and then. Usually I'd head into Veregin or Kamsack. Prohibition was on, but there was bootleg liquor to be had all over the damn place. I was staying in a hotel in Veregin one time, and I was sitting out in the lobby in plain clothes. Some brakemen just off a train came into the lobby and one of them asks me, "Where's the boss?" I told him I didn't know where the hell the boss was, but he must have been a pretty thirsty son of a bitch because he said, "You mind taking down a couple of bottles for us?"

"Well," I said, "that just wouldn't be right if I did." This guy started to look a little pissed off and says, "Why not?" So I just pulled out my badge and showed it to him. He got a little red because he'd just asked a cop to give him bootleg liquor. I had to laugh.

After a couple of months on the Doukhobor trouble, they sent me back to Regina for a couple weeks to finish off basic training. As soon as I was through, I put my application in for Arctic service—that was the main reason I'd joined the force, not to beat up Doukhobors.

Before my application went through they stuck me on border patrol between Saskatchewan and Montana. There was a band of American robbers coming over the border and robbing grain elevators. I guess some high-up figured a couple cops in a new Model A driving back and forth along

Bill's first official picture as a full-fledged constable in the RCMP.

the border might deter the robbers, but we spent more time getting that car out of mudholes than we did actually patrolling.

I had a nice old corporal as my partner in that Model A. One time we were following an old Model T coupe on a paved stretch of road. Every few miles a beer bottle would come flying out of this car, so we figured we'd better pull them over. Both of us walked up the driver's side and saw a big bucket of ice with beer sitting in the back of the car. We pulled it out and this corporal said to me, "You think that's beer?"

"I dunno." We knew damn well what it was. There were labels on the things for chrissakes.

"I guess there's only one sure way to find out," this corporal says. He asks these couple of travellers if they have an opener and the driver says, "Oh yeah sure, here you are," and hands him an opener. We open a beer apiece and knock them back. When we finish, this corporal says, "You think that's beer?" and I say, "No, I don't think so." He turns to these travellers and says, "Okay, you go on. I thought you guys were drinking beer in here."

Another time out on border patrol, I was staying in a hotel in Estevan. I'd been out and about but it was eight or nine o'clock, so I decided to turn in. On the way to my room I saw that the door next to mine was open and that there were a couple of guys in there. "Come on in, come on in," they said. I went in there and they were really tying one on. I figured I'd have a few drinks with them, but they were really pie-eyed. Both were paint salesmen for different companies and they got talking about their various products and started up an argument over whose stuff was better. There was a big bloody dresser there, so one guy got out a can of his paint and he slapped it all over this dresser. Then he grained it with a little graining tool. The other guy said, "That's nothing." So he went and grained a bigger patch on the wall, right on the bloody plaster. They made the goddamnedest mess of that room you ever seen.

I was a few drinks in when one of the salesmen fell over the end of the bed and figured he broke his ribs. He was in pretty bad pain but I couldn't figure out how he'd break his ribs just falling over the bloody bed. I said, "How the hell you break your ribs falling over a bed?"

"Well," he said, "I just busted them ten days ago. Guess I managed to re-break the things." I told him that he better get a doctor, but he wouldn't have it. "You set 'em," he said. It sounded like a bad idea, but I thought if he could stand it I could. He took his shirt off on the bed and I started feeling around his ribs. You could sure as hell tell they were broken. They were kind of sticking up under the skin all over the place. I got my finger on them and shoved down and then pulled some tape over top. It must've hurt like hell, but he was so liquored up that he barely noticed. That put an end to the party.

I saw the guy a couple weeks later. "How's those ribs?" I asked. He said he never had another problem with them.

4

WET FEET

My Arctic application went through pretty quickly. In December of '29 they transferred me out to E Division in Vancouver, where I was supposed to wait for the Arctic schooner *St. Roch* to depart in the spring. I really didn't know what to expect out west. I'd been told they didn't treat the young constables too good out there. One day you could be writing traffic tickets, the next you were doing what we called "bitch jobs." There wasn't a man around who wanted those bitch jobs. They'd have you clean the barracks, answer the phone, work in the kitchen, look after stables—all the kinds of things a young guy just hates.

I got my first introduction to the *St. Roch* crew while I was on phone bitch—answering the phones. My switchboard was right beside a window, and outside the window there was a parking lot. A car pulled up there one day. I didn't get a glimpse of the driver. All I saw was a big arm come out of the driver's window, offering me a silver flask. Well, I thought this guy must be okay, so I grabbed the flask and took a big swig. It damn near took the enamel right off my teeth but I didn't let on. It was straight overproof rum. I handed the bottle back and the driver stuck his head out the window where I could see him.

"I'm Bob Kells," he said. "What kind of gut have you got anyway?" It turned out that Bob Kells was one of the engineers aboard the *Roch*. He was about the best man among them too—a big, good-natured fella who got along well with everyone. He'd been on the first trip up with the *Roch* a year before and gained a lot of respect among the Inuit up there. They had a big flu epidemic up in Herschel Island some time that year. The natives were just dying like flies and Bob packed a lot of them to the graveyard over his shoulder. Those natives really appreciate a thing like that because it wasn't every white man who'd do it.

The RCMP had their barracks at 33rd and Heather. That's where I stayed until the *Roch* came in. We had to keep a night guard there just like back in Regina. I was on guard one night with a Constable Emerson. They were pretty strict about uniform in those days. You had to pass inspection before you went on night duty. Someone figured shiny boots and buttons would keep the commies at bay. As soon as the inspecting officer buggered off, Emmy and I went into the guardroom, where he pulled out a bottle of rum. He said, "That's not for tonight. Tomorrow's

The barracks at 33rd and Heather in Vancouver.

my birthday, so we have to wait until then." I must have been a little thirsty because I said, "We'll have one drink." We had that one drink over a game of cards. Then we had another and another and another until we killed the bloody bottle. Emmy was blotto, and I wasn't feeling any pain myself. He had a key for the canteen, so he stumbled off there to have a snooze. I decided to lie down for a while in one of the cell bunks—didn't have any trouble going to sleep either.

I woke up to the sound of bootsteps. It wasn't any goddamn communist—it was one of the sergeants. I jumped outta bed and there was that empty rum bottle sitting on the table with a couple glasses all in plain view. Smith was this sergeant's name, and he was in charge of the guard. He twigged right away.

He said, "Where the hell is Emerson?"

I knew exactly where he was. "I don't know," I said. "He was here a minute ago."

Smith told me to get my ass out of bed and feed the horses while he looked for Emmy. I did that and when I came back, Smith was there. He'd spotted Emmy through the canteen window, flaked out on the floor. He said, "I can't wake him up and the door's locked." We didn't know what the hell to do. Finally I pried open the window and I went in, woke up Emmy and unlocked the door.

We thought sure as shit we were going to get the goddamn book thrown at us. So Emmy and I got on with our day's work, thinking the whole time we'd get our asses booted out. Emmy came into my room that night to ask if I'd heard anything. "Not a damn peep," I said. Emmy was much older than I was. He had about twelve or fourteen years in by then and he was worried about missing out on pension. Well, it turned out that the old sergeant never said a word.

We got away with everything short of murder down at those barracks. Every afternoon we did stables. We had to parade the horses around and then groom them for a few hours. To break the monotony we used to call up a cab driver and get him to

The stables at the Vancouver barracks.

drop off a couple cases of beer in the bushes across the street from the barracks. We used to slip out on a regular basis and have a few tall, cold ones. Most of us young guys were in on it. Sometimes Sergeant Major Jock Binning, the guy in charge of the whole barracks, would cross the street and try to give us shit. He was a miserable bastard with a face only a blind mother could love. He'd yell, "What the Jesus is going on here?" He knew perfectly well what was going on and we all knew that he was a heavy boozer.

"Oh, we're just having a beer, Sarge," someone would say. "Come and join us." He would grumble a bit, but he always joined in. After two or three drinks he would be almost human.

Starting in the spring, we took the *Roch* out on trials. Now, I may've learned a lot of things in Saskatchewan that served me well in the Arctic, but boating wasn't among them. It was hard to get sea time in Saskatchewan. I had the least experience of anyone on board. The ten-minute trips we took across Burrard Inlet on the little ferry they had there seemed like quite a cruise to me. Anybody watching the *St. Roch* go by during my first few tricks at the wheel must've figured we were taking evasive action.

The training we got aboard the *Roch* while it was in Vancouver was a complete waste of time. Once you learn how to keep the tub straight, there ain't much more to it. But the brass figured

The *St. Roch* on its first trials off Bowen Island, June 1928.

they had to put us through the gauntlet all the same. The guy in charge of E Division in Vancouver was a fella by the name of Newson, but everyone called him Nuisance. He took us out on trials because the captain, Henry Larsen,[6] was taking extended shore leave. Newson's idea of seeing how the *Roch* worked was throwing out four hundred yards of heavy anchor chain and having the crew wind it in by hand—the stupid old bastard. We had to wind in all that anchor line by hand and one guy had to stay below and stow the chain. That was a shits of a job because it would come up all slimy from the bottom. All we needed to do was throw the anchor winch in gear. And we should've, because the old bastard wasn't even watching us. He was sitting there in Henry's cabin while we were winding, and every now and then we'd see a beer bottle fly out the window.

I got to know the crew pretty good before we set off. They were all decent enough guys—aside from Anderton, who none of us liked right from the get-go. He was the sergeant in charge of the *Roch's* policing duties. Henry was just in charge of her sailing duties. You see, the *Roch* was supposed to be a mobile RCMP detachment, and whenever she was performing any kind of police duty, it was Anderton's show. Back then the RCMP was the only official government presence up north. We were responsible for carrying the mail, ferrying Inuit, exploring shipping routes, bringing supplies into the police posts, handing out rations for the destitute—everything. For a guy in charge of all that, Anderton sure made himself scarce all through trials. He just stayed in his cabin. The actual crew was made up of eight men: Bob Kells and Art Jones were the engineers, Dad Parry was

---

6. Henry A. Larsen was born in Norway in 1899. While serving aboard the Arctic trading vessel *Maid of Orleans* from 1924–26, he befriended a number of RCMP constables on Herschel Island, who convinced him that he should enlist in the force. Larsen entered the RCMP in 1927 with the intention of joining the crew of the planned Arctic schooner *St. Roch*. He served as mate on the ship's first voyage north in 1928 and was promoted to captain the next year. He spent over thirty years in the force, retiring in 1961 as officer commanding the Arctic G Division. He died October 29, 1964.

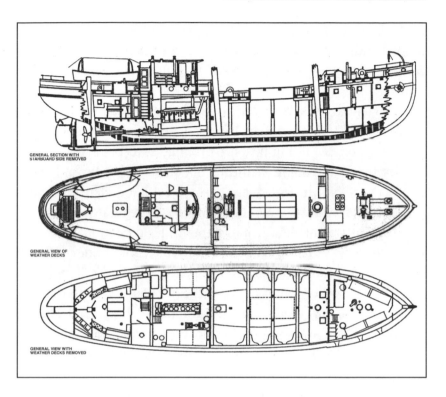

GENERAL SECTION WITH
STARBOARD SIDE REMOVED

GENERAL VIEW OF
WEATHER DECKS

GENERAL VIEW WITH
WEATHER DECKS REMOVED

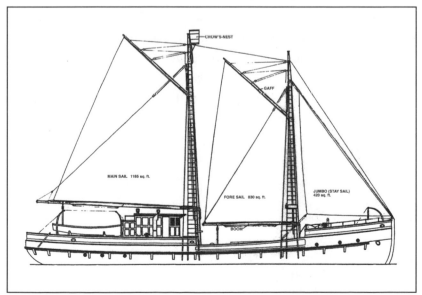

CROW'S-NEST

GAFF

MAIN SAIL 1185 sq. ft.

FORE SAIL 830 sq. ft.

JUMBO (STAY SAIL)
420 sq. ft.

BOOM

Views showing the original layout of the *St. Roch*, before renovation.
Courtesy Vancouver Maritime Museum.

cook, Davies ran the radio, Fred Farrar was mate, and Dinty Moore and I were seamen. Then of course there was Larsen, captain of the ship. He's worked up quite the legend over the years.

Henry had worked under sail and steam since he was a fifteen-year-old kid in Norway. He was just a nice, easy-going guy. He was in the RCMP, but he hadn't trained as a cop. They needed a sailor to operate the *Roch* and Henry was a sailor, he had experience in the North so they took him on. I liked Henry because he was different from the others. More of a regular joe. At least at first. This was his first trip as captain. He'd been mate aboard the *Roch* on its shakedown cruise the year before under Captain Gillen. They found on that first trip that she had a few kinks. They didn't bother fixing most of the problems, though Henry insisted on a few, like getting a new deck winch and anchor windlass. There was only so much they could do. She had a flawed design as far as I could see.[7] You thought the thing was going to capsize in a low swell and she had a puny 150-horsepower Union diesel for power. She barely made six and a half knots in good weather and for some reason she always seemed to be bucking the damn wind everywhere we went. She had three sails too, and Henry would haul them out whenever he could.

Farrar was the only one of us aside from Henry who was a genuine sailor. He once served aboard a passenger liner that ran to Africa. I guess he learned basic navigation there, something the rest of us didn't have.

---

7. By 1927 the RCMP had established seven posts in the Arctic using chartered vessels. They decided then that they needed their own ship in the area to effectively connect and supply the posts, serve as a mobile detachment and assert Canadian sovereignty in the North. Tom Halliday, a Vancouver naval architect who had experience with other police ships, designed the Arctic vessel. She was constructed by Burrard Drydock in North Vancouver, launched May 7, 1928, and named *St. Roch* for the Quebec parish that was federal Minister of Justice Ernest Lapointe's riding. She was hauled ashore for a final time in 1958 and now rests high and dry as the centrepiece of the Vancouver Maritime Museum.

5

ROLLING ON THE *ROCH*

W̶e pulled out of Vancouver in June without much fuss, which was okay by us. A month earlier we made headlines and they weren't good ones. It was one of our last days out on trials and we were all starting to think we were real sailors. There was a Hudson's Bay Company trading ship by the name of the *Old Maid* berthed right ahead of us. She was a nice old ship with a long history as a rum-runner, sealer and black-birder early on.[8] I remember going down in the hold of that ship one time and they still had the shackles

---

8. The *Old Maid* was built in 1882 and was originally used as a "black-birder," smuggling slaves from the islands of the South Pacific to sugar plantations in Queensland and mines in South America under the name *Maid of Orleans*. Around the turn of the century, she was converted to a cod-fishing boat and was one of the most productive boats in the Puget Sound fleet until the fishery collapsed in the early '20s, and she was sold to Charlie Klengenberg. He renamed her the *Old Maid No. 2* and put her to work as an Arctic trader. When Klengenberg retired from Arctic trading in 1928, he sold the ship to the Hudson's Bay Company, who completed two Arctic trips with her before selling her to a rum-running outfit. With prohibition lifted in 1933, she returned to work as an Arctic trader under her original name. In 1936, she lost 50 feet of her keel on a reef during a trip north, but remained afloat. She was salvaged by the lumber baron Gordon Gibson, renamed the *Joan G.* and used as a towboat, fish-packer, freighter and barge. Today, her remains rest on the beach a quarter of the way up the BC coast at Cockatrice Bay on Broughton Island.

The *Roch* sitting at her North Vancouver berth just before heading north.

down there that they'd used to chain up slaves. Henry had actually served on her at one time, when she was owned by a guy by
the name of Charlie Klengenberg. We were on our way into our
berth and just as we come up on the *Old Maid*, Henry rang down
to the engine room for a full stop. Bob Kells, the engineer down
there, thought this was kind of strange but stopped the engine
anyway. Well that silly bugger Henry should have rang for us
to go astern because the engine stopped as we were plowing
forward at a pretty good rate of speed and we coasted right into
the stern of the *Old Maid*—punched a big bloody hole in her
too. Jesus Christ, did Henry ever light up over that one. He was
so goddamn embarrassed. He thought they might take the ship
away from him. And it didn't get any better when the papers
came out the next day. One of them had the headline "Mounties
Ram *Old Maid* In Her Stern." He maintained to his grave that
he didn't ring for the ship to stop, but we saw it happen. The
Old Maid eventually got her stern patched up, but the wound in
Henry's pride took a little longer to heal.

We had good weather the first few days out of Vancouver.
That gave us a bit of a false impression, because the *Roch* seemed
a fine ship when the sun was shining and the wind was calm. We

The *Old Maid* caught in ice a few years before the *St. Roch* punched a hole in her stern. Harbour Publishing archives.

A wave crashes over the gunwale of the *St. Roch* while she cruises through heavy North Pacific seas. The photo also shows how dozens of fuel barrels stored on deck necessitated building a second temporary deck on top of them.

found out what she was really like when we passed the northern tip of Vancouver Island. Instead of going up the Inside Passage like almost anybody else, even much bigger ships, as soon as we got to the top of the Island, Henry made a beeline for the Bering Strait, right across the North Pacific. I remember looking out and seeing what looked like green mountains, except they were moving. The *Roch* stood on her head and stood on her tail and rolled both rails under. The seas broke right over the cargo load out on the bow. We used to have to tie ourselves into bed. We'd tie a rope to the rails on either side of the bunk. You'd just fly out of bed sometimes without that rope. If it was really rough we'd put a rope from the back aft up to the wheelhouse. You'd wait for a wave to crash over and then you'd grab this rope and run to beat hell up to the wheelhouse before the next one crashed over. You could barely keep the boat on course in that kind of weather. The wheel didn't have any power assist or anything, so sometimes it took two of us just to hold her in a straight line.

The *Roch* was designed for Arctic service, you see. She had a rounded hull so that she could rise up on top of the ice when it pressed in. When you have a straight-sided hull, the ice just wedges up against it and it can crush the hull. With her bathtub shape, the *Roch* might have been proof against the ice, but the way she handled on the way there it felt like you were going to capsize long before making it far enough north to see ice. Yes, *Roch* was what she was called and rock was what she did.

The big swells you could get used to after a while; it was those short, sharp ones that were the worst. Some of those waves out in the North Pacific were about a quarter of a mile apart. It was just like going up in an escalator—you just rise, rise, rise, rise and all at once you're sitting up on top and looking down at valleys on both sides and then you start down until you're looking up on both sides. Sometimes the wind would cut the top off the waves and there'd be forty feet of spray above the water. Boy, it stung like gravel when that spray hit your face.

Everyone aside from Henry spent a good deal of time over the rail during the first four or five days at sea. Bob Kells used to say, "One thing we proved is that no matter how weak your stomach is, you can heave just as far as a man with a strong stomach."

Between trips over the rail our cook, Dad Parry, tried to whip up a bit of grub, but in those seas it was hopeless. You couldn't keep a pot in one place for a second before it was flying across the tiny galley he had to work in. We lived off cheese and hardtack those first few days in the open, but none of us had much of an appetite anyway.

By the fourth day in open seas, our stomachs got pretty well back to normal and we fell into a pretty smooth routine. We worked four hours on the wheel, then four hours off, then four more hours on and four more off. Then we'd work a six-hour shift and hit the sack for another six. Me and Farrar worked one shift, Henry and Dinty Moore worked the other.

Farrar and I got along fine doing watch together. I knew him from Regina and thought he was just a son of a bitch then. He'd been in the navy or something and figured that put him way above the rest of us. He was always strutting around saluting and lecturing us rubes on correct military procedure. He was quite a favourite with the higher-ups. We damn near had a rhubarb there one time. There was an Irishman by the name of Paddy Gardner. Farrar lit into Gardner one time when he'd had a few drinks and started dressing him down for being a disgrace to the force or some of his usual crap. Gardner was a big bugger and he wanted to clean Farrar's clock, but a few of the guys held him back. I said, "Let him go. Let the bastard have what he's got coming." They didn't listen, but Farrar came after me and I knocked him right flat on his ass. Then he went to the superiors with some bullshit story and got me put on report. I told some of the guys what had happened, so we put him on the silent treatment. We never spoke a word to him. It was damn effective. The only time he could get anyone to say anything was when he asked them a direct question, and then he'd only get a one-word answer. He'd get lonely sometimes and come over, but we'd all just talk amongst ourselves and ignore him. When I got to Vancouver, Farrar was there waiting to go north too. He had signed on as mate. To give him credit, he came right up to me and said, "Look Bill, I know I wasn't right back there in Regina, but I learned something from it and I'm asking you to give me another chance. We're going to be stuck with each other up north and it'll go a lot easier if we get along." He stuck out his mitt and I took it. Well, from then on we got on just fine. Once we started to trust each other a bit, we made a pretty good team.

On watch, you'd stay on the bridge the whole time. If you were out at sea, you'd stay in the wheelhouse, but if you were near land, you'd go out on deck to keep an eye on things. There wasn't a heck of a lot of socializing down below. Just a bit of bitching over grub, maybe do laundry and then turn in.

One time Kells thought to hell with doing the laundry, and he just tied his greasy overalls on a rope and dangled them off the stern. Well, he came out there next watch and the things were just whipped to threads.

Turning in wasn't always so easy either because, on top of the rocking, the bloody decks all leaked. Why they couldn't caulk them up I don't know. Every section of the boat had water coming in from above if there were rough seas out, and the fo'c'sle really started to get clammy. One morning when Farrar and I were coming off watch the doggone bunks were all wet, so he fired up the coal heater we had in there to try and dry things out. The fo'c'sle wasn't very big, I suppose eighteen feet long and ten feet wide. After running the stove for half an hour, it was like a Turkish bath. I remember seeing Farrar get up and open the little door to let some heat out. It wasn't too rough at that point, but a few hours later I woke up and found the ship was rolling to beat hell. I'll never forget looking up and seeing water pouring through that little doorway in a solid green shaft right into the fo'c'sle. Farrar yelled, "Holy Christ, we've foundered." There was about three feet of water sloshing in the rear part of the fo'c'sle because it was sloped back towards the stern. I scrambled up to the top bunk before I got very wet, but we'd taken in a good thousand gallons and with every pitch of the boat it sluiced from one bulkhead to the other. There was a big tin bucket we had in there and it bowled over everything in its path. One of the things in its way was a collection of paint cans Henry had stowed away. Within a few pitches the water was all the colours of the rainbow.

There was still water slopping in through the door from the deck, and there was danger of another big one coming over the bow, but neither of us felt like enough of a hero to get down in that soup to go close the door, so we just crouched there on our bunks, watching it slosh and getting sick on the fumes. Finally a couple of the guys made it back with a pump and bailed us out, but you never saw such a goddamn mess. There was paint over everything—woodwork, bedding, stove, gear—and the smell of turpentine was so strong it made your stomach heave. There was nowhere else to lie down on that bloody boat and we got too tired to care all that much about the smell so we climbed back into the bunks and went to sleep, but it sure gave you one hell of a headache.

That was in the North Pacific, just a few days before we got into Dutch Harbour on Unalaska Island. Henry had saved a few days by making the straight shot to the Aleutians, but for every day he saved, his green crew must have aged a year. We didn't all know it then, but there was quite a competition to be the first boat into the Arctic after the ice broke, and Henry was making sure he was in good position.

6

DUTCH HARBOUR

After two weeks rolling around inhaling turpentine fumes, Dutch Harbour was sure a welcome sight. There was a radio base for the US Army there and a cannery stocked full of about a hundred girls up from Seattle to work for the summer. I guess there wasn't much to do around Dutch Harbour because they seemed just as eager to meet us as we were to meet them. We barely had time to tie up before a bunch of them swarmed aboard the boat, still wearing the shirts, jeans and hair scarves they worked in. There were girls in the saloon, girls in the galley, girls in the wheelhouse and in the fo'c'sle. There were even a couple up in the crow's nest. I can't say we did much to discourage them.

That night they put on a big dance for us and there was about ten girls for every guy. They were all wearing their best dresses with their hair down. One girl spent a good bit of time with Davies in the radio shack earlier in the day, but he didn't recognize her when she was all dolled up at the dance.

"You've forgotten me already?" she said.

Davies, who was painfully bashful, said, "I'm sorry. I didn't recognize you with your dress on." Everyone got quite a laugh

The *St. Roch* tied up in Dutch Harbour.

A freighter anchored in Dutch Harbour.

out of this and Davies lit up like a tomato. She didn't seem to mind too much. The two of them disappeared together for the rest of the night.

Before we left Vancouver, we went on quite a shopping spree with special permits that gave us necessary commodities tax-free. Cigarettes were $2.50 for a thousand, a gallon of overproof rum was $6, fine Scotch was $22 a case. We couldn't see any better place to invest these assets, so we spent most of our time in Dutch Harbour pretty gowed up.

I guess the local army guys didn't think too much of us poaching on their territory, because a group of them came down to the dock the next morning trying to start something. They made jokes like "How many screws on that there boat," and so on. There's nobody in the world as mouthy as Yanks in a gang like that. They said if we wanted to show our mettle we had to box them. They had one big bastard there with gloves on and they were waving another pair around for one of us to throw on. Now I've never been one to sit out on a good tussle, but this guy was a monster—at least 250 pounds and built like a linebacker.

Well, we all just kinda looked at each other wondering which

Bill sitting with new friends. Sitting with him in the front row are, from left to right, Fred Farrar, Jim Davies and Art Jones.

Jim Davies, radio operator and "one tough monkey."

one was going to volunteer to get the shit-kicking, when Davies stepped out of the radio shack and said, "I'll try." Davies was just a squirt of a guy, easily the smallest on the crew. We figured all that romancing had gone to his brain, but Christ, none of us were about to step in, so up the ladder he went with the pair of gloves. "Too small, too small! Throw the little one back! Give us a man!" they hollered.

Well, Davies could've killed that big bastard. Jesus, he was good. Just jab, jab, jab, get the guy backed up, then whistle a trip-hammer past his chin—Davies could easily have hit him but he was just playing with him. That big fella hardly got a punch off. Those Yanks quieted right down. We were just as surprised as they were. Davies was always such a quiet guy. I got talking to him after and found out he'd been a pug. He'd fought many, many fights. He was one tough monkey, but you never would have suspected it.

We actually got to be pretty good friends with those army guys, and the rest of the trip was pretty much a contest to drink everything on the entire island. On the last night, me and Bob Kells stumbled up to the army wireless station with two of the operators, Tobin and Chicago. We had a good game of cards going until we ran out of booze. Chicago got so thirsty he started skimming the scum off a batch of green homebrew he had sitting there. We were just about to call it a night when a couple Swedes came in with a bottle of this Alaska Mule, which is called that because it kicks like one. Well, we decided it wouldn't be polite to leave then. Kells was usually a good-natured fellow, but after a couple drinks of this Alaskan Mule he turned ornery. He had his chair leaning back against the wall on two legs, and he said to these two Swedes, "You guys better fuck off."

Nobody paid any attention to him and we carried on for another five minutes or so until he said again, "You guys better fuck off." Still no action. Finally he says, "I told you guys to fuck off and you didn't, so I'm going to throw you out." There was an army cot there, the kind with angle iron rails. Kells leaned forward on the chair. The chair stopped, but old Bob didn't. He kept pitching forward and dove right under the bed. As he went under, he contacted some angle iron and it clipped a patch of scalp about the size of a silver dollar off the back of his head. We picked him up and put him in a bed upstairs. He was bleeding to beat hell. We wrapped the sheets around his head and the blood soaked right through them.

Again I thought I'd better call it a night, but Chicago said, "Let's wreck the fucking joint." By God, we turned that wireless station right upside down. First we tried to turn over the pool table, but it was too heavy. We moved on to busting up chairs and using the legs to smash out all the windows. We picked up everything that wasn't bolted to the floor and threw it out the windows or against the walls. Then we started this goddamn game in the kitchen. The walls were lined with donnacona, a kind of cheap pulp board, and the game was to see what you could throw through the wall. Christ, we threw plates and pans and knives. The meat cleaver went through without even slowing down. One guy put an alarm clock through the wall and we went out to look and the son of a bitch was still ticking. Finally

Bill holding a halibut caught off the stern of the boat with a handline in Dutch Harbour.

we ran out of things to throw, and somehow I found my way back to the boat. Pie-eyed as I was, I knew we were going to leave first thing next morning.

Old Henry, he was down at the boat trying to round up the crew, but he couldn't find Kells. So he went ashore to the wireless station and saw this goddamn wreck up there. It was really a shambles. At any rate he went upstairs and found Bob in bed with all the sheets soaked in blood. Bob was still out cold.

Henry came back all shit hot and hollered, "Roll out, roll out, you guys. Someone's beat the piss out of Bob. They damn near killed him. We'll go ashore and show them cocksuckers what it's all about." He was ready to start a war. I figured I better tell him what'd happened before he did anything too drastic. "Oh," he said, "we better get out of here before they come looking for us." He got a couple of the guys together and they dragged Bob back down.

In the morning Bob didn't remember a goddamn thing about it. He figured he'd been in a fight. He remembered I'd been there and asked, "Some son of a bitch must have hit me with a bottle. Who was it?" I wouldn't give him any satisfaction. I just put him off. He said, "You son of a bitch. Who the hell you covering up for? I wanna know." Finally I said, "It was no bottle, Bob. You don't know how lucky you are. That bloody guy swung at you with a meat cleaver. You ducked just in time. He would've taken your bloody head off."

His wound healed, but it left a shiny round scar you couldn't help but notice. A couple years later I heard someone ask him, "Jesus Christ, Bob, what happened to your head?"

"Oh I got into a little beef with a guy down there in Dutch Harbour," he said. "Bastard took a swing at me with a meat cleaver. I just ducked in time." He thought that to the day he died.

Henry got away good and early. We were half expecting someone to shoot at us, but we never heard anything more about it. I guess they just blamed it on the Alaska Mule.

7

RACING TO HERSCHEL ISLAND

I guess we had good wind coming out of Dutch Harbour because I remember Henry wanting to "get the rags up." The *Roch* couldn't sail worth a damn, but Henry was a keen sailor and he had the sails up any chance he got. We'd put the sails up a few times out on trials and on the way up. The first few times were fun and the whole crew helped out, but with the sails up you needed men out on the deck to fight the rigging and a steersman who knew what he was doing. It was hard bloody work, and with her bathtub lines you couldn't see any difference the sails made in the *Roch's* speed. It got to be where Henry damn near had to face a mutiny every time he mentioned the subject. I didn't mind so much. It was better than listening to stale BS in the saloon. If there was any wind up I'd say, "Hey Skipper, don't you think we're missing out on some good air here?" Moore and Farrar would just glare, but there was no stopping Henry if he had one friend on his side, and a moment later we'd be out hoisting canvas.

If there was any work needed up aloft, Henry would come and get me whether I was on watch or not. Moore and Farrar were supposed to be sailors but neither of them would climb.

Farrar would only go as far as the crow's nest. Any work higher I had to do. More than once old Henry came and got me out of bed just to send me up the rigging.

Somewhere just out of Dutch Harbour we had a good wind behind us, so Henry decided to show us what the sails could really do and goose-winged them out both sides. The old tub was really moving then, but running wing-on-wing like that is bloody dangerous. Unless you keep the wind dead astern, she'll jibe—one sail will slam around the other side like a door caught in a draft and it can rip the mast right out of the boat. It can be done safely enough, even in a ship that bounced around like we did, but the guy on the wheel had to be on the bit. Normally only Henry would do it, but it was Moore's watch this time and he wanted to prove to everybody what a great sailor he was. He stayed on the wheel while Henry just watched him and looked nervous. You could tell damn well that Henry wanted the wheel, but he had trouble asserting himself. All these stories about his bold Viking blood are just bull.

Moore did all right until the wind really kicked up. He got up on a big roller and the ship yawed till we were taking the wind beam on. The mainsail crashed around and I thought the mast was going to rip right out of the deck. I slacked the sheets and Henry finally got up the courage to grab the wheel from Moore. He swung her about and went up to inspect the damage. The shrouds had held and the mast was okay, but the collar that the halyard was anchored to had been twisted right sideways on the mast, so that when the boom was brought back straight, the block fouled. This collar had four eyes on it, one for the halyard that pulls the sail up and down, and the other three to anchor the stays that held the mast. When we jibed, the whole collar made about a quarter turn and just screwed down into the mast wood. In order to turn it back straight we first had to take the weight of the stays off it with a temporary block hung higher up, and then shim it back in the right position. This meant climbing up to the small part of the mast above the shrouds and clinging

The St. Roch under sail. Bill is in the foreground with Art Jones leaning on the boom behind him.

there with one hand and trying to work with the other. The mast on the *Roch* was sixty feet high, and all the time the boat was pitching in heavy seas. I remember thinking this was a good thing because if I slipped I'd be thrown well into the water rather than cracking my head open on the deck.

I can laugh at that now, but when I think about hanging off that mast or getting sick on turpentine fumes, it makes me wish I could have had a few words with the guy who built that boat. I took so many pinches and cuts and bruises on that damn boat that it still hurts. She seemed to be built to give maximum discomfort. The floor always got half your cup of coffee, there was always a bolt wherever you went to lay your head—even when she was tied up you'd always be stubbing your toe or backing into a sharp edge. Henry, who came closer to loving the *Roch* than anyone, said she was the crankiest, most awkward ship he'd ever set foot on. She'd save your ass in the ice though.

Three days out of Dutch Harbour and bound for the Bering Straits, the weather got pretty miserable. It was completely overcast and I guess Henry couldn't get a sight on the stars to fix our position, but if he and Farrar had any worries, they didn't let on.

As mate, Farrar shared responsibility for navigating. Well, those damn fools just about killed us.

When you're navigating at night you can't see anything, she's pitch black outside. You relied on Henry to lay out the course, taking into account the tides and drift and everything. All you'd stare at was the compass. It was nearing the break of day and Farrar came in to spell me off the wheel. I headed outside for a breather and I noticed that the water looked a little off—it was kind of dirty. I didn't think too much of it, but I had a gut feeling, so I climbed up to the crow's nest. Well, not more than a quarter mile off, there was surf breaking on a low, dark spit and we were heading full speed straight for it.

I yelled at Farrar to bring the ship about. Farrar swung around just in time. A few minutes more and we would've been aground. Henry was sleeping in his cabin right behind the wheelhouse and the change in the ship's motion woke him up. He came storming in and went straight to the compass before saying a word. Now, usually Henry was fairly quiet, but his temperature came up fast if he found the boat was off course. He turned to Farrar and yelled, "What the hell you steering that course for?"

Farrar still really didn't know what the hell was going on, so he said, "Bill told me to put it about." Henry stormed outside to where I was and got right in my face and shouted, "What the hell's the idea?"

I said, "You planning to make a portage over that piece of land back there?"

"Portage? What the hell you talking about? There's no land within a hundred miles of here."

"You climb up and take a look and tell me that."

Henry climbed up on the stays still piping mad. He came down a lot calmer. He said, "You saved the ship, Bill."

We would've rammed into Cape Mohican on Nunivak Island and it'd be game over for the old *Roch*. There was a heavy sea and she'd have pounded her bottom out in a matter of minutes. It was a damn good thing Farrar and I had started working together so well—he didn't question my judgment for a second when I yelled at him. Up until then my lack of experience was the butt of a lot of jokes—"plowboy" they used to call me. The jokes stopped after Cape Mohican. I figured I'd pretty well paid for my passage. Henry chose to forget that incident later on. I bumped into him when I was out of the force.

"Hey Henry, you remember that time I saved the ship?" I asked him.

"No, Bill, I don't remember that," he said. He was always touchy on the subject of his own screw-ups, was Henry.

He wrote a book called *The Big Ship* some years later about his years on the *Roch* and he doesn't remember damn near losing the ship there, either. He remembered a lot of crap that never did happen, though. He has one story in there about how a fresh recruit from the Prairies came running up on deck to shoot a whale during our first few days in open seas, carrying a loaded shotgun and wearing "nothing but his union suit, flap open, face covered with three days' beard and still pale but with the look of the hunter in his eyes." He writes that he had to tell me I couldn't kill a whale with a shotgun and that I went back down below "somewhat dashed."

That's pure cock-and-bull. He can get away with calling me a green cop, but I knew more about guns and hunting than Henry did. If I was gonna shoot at a goddamn whale I would've brought up my .303 rifle. You can stop a whale if you hit them in the spine, but it's a hard shot to make. I knew that and that's why I'd never waste my time shooting from the deck of the *Roch*— the way she rolled, there was no way to get a clean shot at the spine.

Not long after Cape Mohican we started into the ice. At first it was just the odd berg floating around, then all the water turned into slush. That slush told you the pack was close by. All of a sudden you could feel the tension mount among the crew. Anderton, of course, was completely oblivious to the sailing of the ship and just went about his merry way as if on a pleasure cruise, but the rest of us were bloody nervous.

As soon as you get up that far you sure realize that you're in an alien place. It's all low-lying land along the Alaska coast from Nome on up. We stopped in Nome but had to anchor about a mile out. It's all shallow beach with huge surf around there, and we couldn't see how we were going to get ashore in our little lifeboat, until a group of natives paddled out in umiaks to bring us in. The umiaks were open walrus-skin boats that'd fit a dozen or so guys.

Paddling into shore, I couldn't figure out how the hell they were going to land the umiak without flipping her ass over tea-kettle. There were about ten paddlers in the boat. They got nice and close to the shore, watching the rollers, holding the boat back until they saw a big one. Just as it hit the stern of the boat, one guy who was in charge yelled and they all dug their paddles in and kept right on top of that bloody big roller. It lifted us right up on the beach. Then the wave gave out and they stuck their paddles in the ground to hold the boat in place while the wave ran back down. Then we jumped out and everyone grabbed the umiak and ran to beat hell up the beach before the next roller came crashing in.

That technique for landing the umiak was pretty common around that area. We made stops in Wainwright, Cape Prince of Wales, Teller and a few other settlements, and it was the same with the natives and their umiaks in every one. We made all these short stops mainly for dog feed. We were set to bring twenty or twenty-five dogs on board at Herschel Island, so we needed all the cheap seal and dried fish we could get our hands on. We did have some kind of powdered dog food on board, but you had to boil it up and it smelled horrible. That's one son of a bitch of a job, cooking up feed for so many dogs. It was a hell of a lot easier just tossing them a piece of raw seal. Seals are the best dog food you can get. Only drawback to feeding them seal and fish is the bastards start to fart and stink, holy

The crew of the *St. Roch* on shore at Wainwright mingling with Inuit around a small umiak.

Christ. Sometimes when we were going into the wind it would just about turn your gut.

We tried hunting our own feed, but we never had time to do it properly. Somewhere around the Diomede Islands we ran into a huge herd of migrating female fur seals. There were thousands of the things. I guess the bull had gone through about a month earlier and established a breeding territory out on the Diomedes. Those seals put on quite a show for us. They would swim straight for us and start leaping up out of the water, flipping on their backs and clapping their flippers. At night you could see them charging around under water by the glow of the phosphorescence. I tried pegging off as many as I could, but Henry hated having to swing the boat around just to pick up a dead seal.

It was around there that I saw my first walrus, so I went down and grabbed the thirty-ought-six. Walruses are big and they just hang around the edge of the ice all the time. This one was lying on an ice pan about two hundred yards off. You're supposed to shoot them in the back of the head, but I couldn't get a good look. I shot for his head but I hit him right at the base of the tusk. We just saw this white powder shoot up and disintegrate in the air. He slipped into the water pretty quick after that. I didn't kill him, but I gave him a hell of a toothache.

Now Henry may've had his faults, but there's few you'd rather have at the wheel when it came to weaving through ice. Ice makes polar waters the most dangerous in the world, but Henry seemed to have the knack for knowing when to drive into the pack and when to run for shelter. If there was ice around, he'd stay up in the crow's nest for hours on end looking for pathways through it.

Henry and the *Roch* were a good team. She was solid as a rock. That egg-shaped hull saved the crew's bacon more than once. In 1937, a couple years after I left the Arctic, Henry came through Dolphin and Union Strait alongside the Hudson's Bay ship *Fort James*, when a northwester pushed a bunch of heavy ice in from the open sea. The *Roch* popped up and rolled over on top of the ice, but the *Fort James* had a deep, straight-sided hull. The ice closed in and she got crushed.

An American ship passes the *Roch* near the Diomede Islands.

Point Barrow sits right at the most northerly tip of Alaska. That's where the ice pack bottlenecks every summer when it breaks up and floats west. Every spring boats line up below Barrow waiting to make the first run of the season to Herschel Island, which at that time was the major trading centre in the Western Arctic. The big thing was you had to get through that bottleneck early. Later on in the summer the ice would move quite a ways offshore and there'd be a clear passage, but it'd plug up again by September, so if a ship wanted to get much done and still make it out she'd have to fight the ice early. The trading ships had another motive in racing up there because the first ship into Herschel got the best prices. Now the *Roch* wasn't a trading vessel, but Henry wanted bragging rights to being the first skipper into Herschel just as bad as any of them.

Three ships were already waiting below Barrow when we pulled in. There was the Hudson's Bay Company flagship the *Bay Chimo*, the Canalaska Trading Company's *Patterson* and our old friend the *Old Maid*. The *Chimo* was reigning champion of the Herschel race. She wasn't designed for Arctic service. She was a German ship captured during the First World War, with a regular V-shaped steel hull. Her biggest advantage was she always kept an ice pilot aboard—that and the fact her skipper, Sidney Cornwall, had so many bets riding on his getting to Herschel first that he couldn't afford to lose. He never even considered the *Roch* in the running because Henry was in his first year of skippering her.

There was no way we were faster than the other boats, but the *Roch* had a draft of only fourteen feet and Henry took full advantage of it. Most of the land between Barrow and Herschel is low, with very shallow, sloping beaches, and the ice would usually ground a few hundred feet offshore. That left a narrow channel the *Roch* could navigate through, while the bigger ships waited for openings out in deeper water.

A depth sounder back then was an eight-pound hunk of round lead with a dimple in the bottom and a jeezly long piece

The *St. Roch* enters Arctic waters. The crewman on deck is pulling up the heavy lead line.

of rope tied to it. You swung this thing around a few times and then tossed it a good fifteen feet ahead of the boat so that it'd be sitting on bottom by the time the boat caught up to it. The rope had strands of leather woven into it at one, two, three, five, ten and twenty fathoms. The guy on the rope would yell whatever reading he got to Henry. We'd be scraping bottom in anything less than three fathoms. Henry always liked to keep about six fathoms down there, and you couldn't blame him either. That bottom would sometimes jump up on you.

I spent a lot of miserable hours on that lead line. We were in shallow water the whole trip around Barrow, and the only thing that stopped the *Roch* from going up on the rocks was the guy on the lead. You'd toss that thing a few times and get so dog-gone tired you'd feel like you were lifting a cannonball out of the water. And the water up there, oh she's cold. There'd be a roostertail coming off that line as you pulled it in and it'd piss all over you. After an hour or so your hands wouldn't move. The skin on them would be cracked from all the salt and chafing. You couldn't take that for more than an hour at a time, so you went out there in short shifts.

I was new to the ice pack and it was an absolute mystery to me. An ice man like Henry could see the wind and the tide in the way the ice moved, but it's a damn frightening thing for someone who doesn't understand it. Sometimes we'd anchor to grounded ice floes while the main pack went grinding by only a few yards away. There isn't a boat in the world even today that could withstand the full force of a few million tons of ice pinching its hull. The way it moves along slowly and then buckles up is the same way mountains are formed. Christ, you'd see chunks the size of hockey arenas just flip right up in the air. The old *Roch* may've been a good ice boat, but she didn't stand a chance if we got caught in the wrong spot.

We made good progress in that shallow water and you could tell Henry was starting to think we had a chance of beating the *Chimo*. He had a quiet determination in the way he'd scour up and down the pack looking for leads.

Dense fog rolled in just as we were rounding Point Barrow itself—the worst spot for ice. It got to where we could see no more than a few yards ahead. For several days we'd just probe the ice real slow, kind of feeling our way into leads. Sometimes we got lucky and advanced for a few miles and then she would start to close like a vise and we'd have to run to beat hell back to

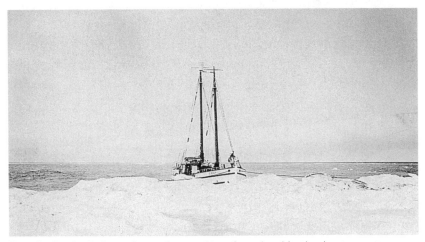

The *St. Roch* anchored to a floe waiting for a lead in the ice to open up.

open water. You couldn't see much but you could sure hear that bloody ice crack and groan and squeak. You didn't know what the hell it was doing out there, but it sure kept a guy from wanting to push his luck.

I started thinking Henry had lost his mind the way he poked up and down the floes looking for these leads. I figured maybe he was risking the boat just to win a race. But I guess old Henry knew what he was doing out there. Sometimes we'd see a lead wide enough to take the *Roch* sideways and he wouldn't go near it. The rest of us would kinda look at each other, then we'd see that big bloody lead clamp right shut.

For a few watches it looked like we weren't going to get anywhere. All the leads had clamped shut. Then we heard the sound of another diesel in the distance and a few minutes later, quite a ways out from us, there was the bloody lights on the *Chimo*. You could see her working through that ice out there pretty quick too. Well, this sure let the steam out of Henry. He figured this inshore route he was navigating would get us a good lead on the other ships. I was more than a little pissed off myself, thinking maybe all that misery with the lead line had been for nothing.

About that time a small lead opened up. Henry charged down her for a few miles until it looked like there was a dead end, but

The *Old Maid* cruising off the *Roch's* starboard as both ships enter ice off Point Barrow.

he just waited for a bit and, wouldn't you know it, the ice jogged off and opened up another little sliver of a lead. It wasn't too long before we were in so far there was no way of getting out, but the ice in front kept opening at the last minute, giving us these skinny leads that the *Roch* barely fit through. Most of the time Henry was a quiet guy none of us took too serious, but God Almighty, he held our lives in his hand out there and everyone but him just stared wide-eyed into the fog. Little by little this lead got wider. The tension was easing up.

Finally Henry said, "We've got 'er," and Point Barrow was behind us.

Henry perked up enough for us to tell that we were back in the race. We hit a bit of open water and the fog lifted, so Henry rang for full speed. It got to be a hell of a nice day out too. There wasn't a piece of ice in sight for quite a few hours. But Henry figured there was more up ahead. He could see what they call "ice blink." That's where you see a light in the sky up ahead caused by the sun reflecting off the ice. Sure enough, we hit another pack within a few hours, right off the Flaxman Islands, halfway to Herschel, and Henry started the old routine of idling up and down the edge of the pack looking for a break. By this time we

The *Roch* navigating leads. A crew member, probably Henry Larsen, scouts a route in the ice from the crow's nest.

were all caught up in thoughts of beating the *Chimo*. We had no idea where the hell she was. She could've been pulled up in Herschel already for all we knew, but we figured we'd got into pretty good shape. Everyone was out there for a spell on the lead line—except Anderton of course.

Bit by bit the ice started to get thinner. There wasn't nearly as much as there was off Barrow. At one point all that separated us from open water was a narrow length of ice, about forty feet wide. Farrar and I came on watch and Henry said we had to keep cruising up and down waiting for a lead. We did this for a couple hours until that little forty-foot section got too hard to ignore.

Finally Farrar said, "The hell with this, let's hit it at that thin spot." I was on the wheel so I circled her back about a quarter of a mile and then ran for all she was worth into that thin spot. She struck pretty hard, slid up on the ice and then laid over hard on one side. The *Roch* was designed for Arctic service, but not as an icebreaker, and I tell you there was a few tense bloody moments sitting up on that ice before she busted through. It was smooth sailing from there on to Herschel.

Coming around the bend toward Herschel the whole crew started climbing up to see if the *Chimo's* big mast was in the dock. There were a few other masts, but none tall enough for the *Chimo*. Henry started leaning on the whistle and holy Christ, by the time we rolled in every man, woman and child was down on the beach shouting and waving. We won—quite an accomplishment for a rookie skipper and a green crew.

8

THE FRIGID FRONTIER

First thing we did in Herschel after putting the anchor down was get on the radio and give the police base at Aklavik the good news. Cornwall was still out there on the ice somewhere and he managed to pick up our signal. That must have pissed him off royally, because not long after, he busted a blade off his propeller trying to get free. There were no drydocks up there so the silly bastard had to spend the rest of the season limping around at half speed.

Cornwall was prone to getting hot-tempered about things. One time I remember him pulling into Coppermine and wanting to go fishing. He considered himself a great fisherman, inquired everywhere he went if there was good fishing around. He wanted to fish in the mouth of the Coppermine River because the char were running. He sat there and fished with one of the local guys but he couldn't get a single goddamn bite. They were there for hours. Right when he was getting to the end of his patience, an Inuit fisherman came down the river in a little boat—he'd just been fishing his nets upriver. This guy motioned to Cornwall that he'd give him a fish. So Cornwall cast his line into the boat and the fisherman hooked on a nice size char that

The *St. Roch, Bay Chimo, Old Maid* and *Patterson* tied up on Herschel Island.

was still alive and dropped it over the side. I guess Cornwall was pretty happy about that until he heard this Inuit let out a big whoop a little ways downstream. That fisherman had landed a gigantic char. Well, old Cornwall was mad as hell, chucked that free char right back in the river.

Now we'd caused the poor bugger to lose all his bets and a propeller blade. To say the least, he was none too happy with Henry when he finally limped into Herschel the next day. At first sight of Henry he yelled, "Goddamn you. You had no business diving into that ice like that. You didn't even know where you were in that fog. You don't know enough to know how bloody lucky you are." Old Henry just beamed a big smile and said he wouldn't let it happen again. By that night Cornwall cooled off a bit and invited Henry over for some Hudson's Bay rum.

There was always a festive feeling when the first boats came in, and it didn't take long for bad moods to be washed away with booze. There were trappers from hundreds of miles around all sitting around there waiting for the boats to get in so they could trade their catches and pick up their orders, and damn near every one of them made sure of getting a full twelve-bottle liquor ration. There was one hell of a drunk. They couldn't get the *Chimo* unloaded for another two days. At one point Henry said he saw Cornwall dancing a jig outside his cabin dressed only in a nightshirt.

The next year up there Cornwall got careless again. He hit the ice off Barrow and the *Chimo* got caught in the middle of a bottleneck. She had quite a few furs on board too. They didn't unload her because they figured she was going down. When the ice is moving and grinding the last thing you'd be worried about is saving a bunch of furs.

Not long after, a few Inuit went out with their dogs and a whaleboat to see what they could salvage off the *Chimo*. It must have been tough going to get out to her. Where they came to water, they loaded the dogs and sled in the boat. Where there was ice, they put the boat on the sled. They managed to get somewhere between twenty and thirty bales of white fox pelts off the *Chimo*. There'd be a hundred foxes in a bale at around twenty bucks apiece, so they done pretty good.

A couple years later, in '33, the captain of the *Patterson* sent me a letter. He said that he'd seen the *Chimo* sitting in good shape on top of a big ice pan. For some years after that, wandering Inuit would bump into the ship floating around like some frozen *Flying Dutchman* of the North. The ice pack doesn't all melt, you see. The bulk of it stays and just circulates around year after year. The *Chimo* may still be drifting around on floes for all I know.

Right in the midst of the big drunk a pod of beluga swam into the harbour. Those Inuit got mighty excited about that. Beluga were among the most prized game up in the Arctic, so everyone who could stand grabbed a rifle, staggered down to the beach and opened fire. A few of them even jumped into little outboard boats and ran back and forth across the harbour mouth to fence the whales in. I was definitely a member of this whale hunt and I definitely used a bloody rifle. I was one of the few who actually hit one too.

After the hunt I stayed down on the beach with a Canalaska trader by the name of Eric Craig. He was from a top-notch Irish family—educated at Oxford and all the rest—and he was the thirty-second pilot shot down by the Red Baron in World War I. He was a real gentleman and a hell of a nice guy, not a bit quarrelsome. He was well off at that time from a good season of trading on Read Island. There was a story behind his good fortune. Craig said that a Church of England preacher sledded into Read Island late the year before, wanting to give a sermon to the Inuit there. This preacher, Webster was his name, had a bad reputation. An Inuit who guided for him a lot said that Webster used to get really mad at the dogs and that one time he grabbed one and chewed its ear off. In other ways he was typical of preachers up there—he didn't speak a word of Inuit and just planned to lecture the natives on their sinful way of life using an interpreter. He had no respect for them at all. The natives were all gathered in Read Island to trade when Webster came in, but they hadn't started yet. Webster asked Craig if he could borrow his interpreter for the sermon, and I guess Craig saw an opportunity because he said yes, but gave the interpreter some instructions beforehand. Webster got up before a fair-sized bunch of natives with this interpreter, and everything Webster said the interpreter translated as "You're all going to go to hell for sure if you don't bring all your fur to Eric Craig." Well, Craig had his best season ever.

Craig and I were just sitting on the beach shooting the shit when Pete Norberg came along. They called him Kogmalik Pete because he had been a trader out east and at the time they called the eastern tribes the Kogmaliks, which means "far away people." They were a different tribe but spoke the same language. Pete was drunk, and when he got drunk he was always looking for trouble.

Pete started trying to pick a fight with Craig, who put it off and ignored it until he couldn't ignore it any more. Hell, Craig just beat the bloody Jesus out of him. Pete didn't stand a show. Craig was a good boxer. He'd taken it up when he went to Oxford. Finally old Pete had enough and he raced straight for the water.

I don't know what he was thinking. He just started to swim out there, and he was a good swimmer. The water was ice cold you know, but he kept going straight away from shore. I thought he might end up drowning himself, so I got in a boat with a couple of guys and we rowed up to him, but the silly old bugger didn't want to get in the boat—he kept swimming away. We finally hauled him in and took him over to the *Chimo*. The only way to get up on deck was a Jacob's ladder,[9] and do you think he would climb that thing? No chance. He said, "Put the goddamn boom over and winch me aboard." The guys on the deck swung the boom over, dropped a line down and then started to winch him up. He got about ten feet from the deck and decided he didn't want to go aboard any more, so he let go and dropped straight down into the water until he disappeared. Christ, the water was so clear around there that you could see about seventy-five feet down, but we couldn't see him. I figured the old bastard really had it this time. A minute later or so we heard thrashing on the other side of the *Chimo*. The crazy bastard went clean down one side of the hull and up the other. That was no easy feat, the *Chimo* must've drawn at least twenty feet of water. He still said he didn't want to come aboard, but finally changed his mind when we promised him some hot rum. But hell, swimming in that freezing water I don't know how he didn't kill himself. If he'd been sober he wouldn't have lasted five minutes.

Norberg was quite a character. He'd mined gold in Australia and the Klondike and he'd been around the Horn three times. He came to the Arctic as a whaler and decided to stick it out as a trader. In 1924 he started the first trading post on King William Island. He owned a small motor scow that he called the *Hobo* and a twenty-ton sailing ship called the *El Sueño*. He and another guy loaded twenty ton of trading goods on this sailboat and a few more on this little scow and started out for King William Island towing the *El Sueño*. Christ, that must have been slow

---

9. A Jacob's ladder is a rope ladder with wooden steps.

going. When the winds were good they switched places on the tow rope and the *El Sueño* towed the *Hobo*. They made it eventually and set up a post that kept running for years after they were dead and gone.

There were a lot of real characters like Pete and Craig hanging around Herschel. Old Bill Seymour was another one. He was seventy and stood about six foot four with a stoop. He had the biggest hands of any man I've ever seen—they were like post mauls. He was about as tough as his hands were big; even at his age, no one dared cross him. He'd been boss of the entire whaling fleet, and one time in Hawaii he boxed to a draw with Tom Sharkey, who was a challenger to the world's heavyweight championship. Bill wasn't a boxer or anything, he was just one tough bastard.

Seymour's daughter came in on the *Chimo* that season. You never saw someone look so out of place. She was dressed in the fanciest damn clothes, just like she was still parading around downtown Vancouver. Within a day or two a bit of a cold snap hit and she was back in an arthcgi [parka] and mukluks [seal-skin boots] just like everyone else. A few weeks later, while we were in Bernard Harbour, she pulled in and married an Alaskan trapper by the name of Patsy Weyant. They had one hell of a party but they never stayed together very long. She couldn't handle being away from civilization much.

Whalers like Seymour had to be bloody well tough. I had a friend around Herschel named Rudolph Johnson who'd been a special constable for many years up there and had seen the whaling in its heyday. He had the job of taking mail from Aklavik to Herschel Island. One time on the mail route he was crossing part of the Mackenzie Delta. Way in the distance he could see what looked like a dog team out on the sea ice. When he got closer he could see it was a bunch of men hooked to a sled just like dogs, with the mates driving them. Rudolph said the way they had them hooked up looked just like they were driving dogs. These guys had been frozen in around Shingle Point, about fifteen miles from Herschel, and were scrounging drift-wood that'd floated down the Mackenzie to use for fuel.

When Rudolph got to Herschel he stayed for about a week on one of the whaling ships. At the time, most whalers wintered at Herschel and there could be four or five hundred men staying there any given winter. One morning aboard the ship he was on, a mate sent one of the crew down into the hold to get something. The hold was quite deep. This crewman went down the ladder without a light and he couldn't find whatever the mate sent him for. He came back up the ladder until his head was just above the top of the hatch. He looked up at the mate and said he couldn't find the thing. The mate said, "Get back down there and take an-other look" and kicked the crewman right in the face. He knocked the fellow right off the ladder and he fell down on a timber at the bottom of the hold and broke his back. Just before Rudolph left, the guy died. A man's life wasn't worth anything.

There was still a whaling station in Dutch Harbour when we were there. They landed 3,700 whales that year. You'd see these killing boats come in towing one or two whales. They'd kill them with bomb-tipped harpoons shot out of a cannon. The gunner put a shot into the whale and the bomb went off about three sec-onds later. It'd make the whale bleed to death. Then they'd shove

The whaling station on Unalaska Island.

a sharp rod in the whale and blow it up with steam so that it'd float, put a flag in it and go after a few more whales. When they had enough they fastened all these whales together and pulled them in. At Dutch Harbour they had a big U-shaped ramp about a hundred feet across with winches on both sides that would pull the whale right up into the centre. Once the whale was in place on this ramp, guys with caulk boots and long, curved knives jumped up on the whale, cut a toggle hole and hooked it up to one of the winches. That made it so the winch could rip all the skin off. The whole village would come down and cut pieces out of this big sheet of skin. You'd see the pieces going in every direction. They regarded the outer skin, the muktuk, as a real delicacy. Some up there made ice houses just so they could keep that muktuk year round. I always thought the best part was the pink layer just under the skin.

Whale used to be a big part of the Inuit diet, but not any more. I have to laugh about the stories that come out so often about whales getting stuck under the winter ice. The media plays it for all it's worth, and banks spearhead rescue funds and all the rest. In the old days a whale getting stuck in the ice was the best thing that could happen for the Inuit. They relied on stranded whales for thousands of years. Sometimes that was the only thing that kept them from starving in the winter.

It was nearing the end of the big whaling fleets when I was up there, but there was still lots of whales around. I remember one morning waking up on the *Roch* and seeing whales in every direction. You could see spouts about every quarter mile. Eventually they swam upwind of us—talk about halitosis. They go down for about half an hour and by the time they come up that air is pretty rotten. Damn near knocked a guy out cold.

Leaving Herschel wasn't easy. Being the first boat in, they treated us pretty well around there. But after several days everyone was starting to sober up and part ways. We took on some dogs, diesel and another constable by the name of Jack McRae, and headed east for Baillie Island.

9

KLINKY

Before we left Vancouver I'd gotten to know one of the most notorious of those old whalers. Charlie Klengenberg was his name. He'd moved down to North Vancouver from the Arctic and he'd come aboard the *Roch* regularly. I didn't know it at the time, but he was something of a living legend in the North. You heard stories about old Klinky everywhere you went up there. Most of them were bad and most of them were true, according to the old-timers.

Old Klinky was born in Denmark and, like most white old-timers up there, he came to the Arctic aboard a whaling ship around the turn of the century. He seized one of these ships in 1904 and sailed it east from Herschel to Victoria Land. I guess him and an engineer on the boat didn't see eye to eye, because they had a gunfight one morning and the engineer was badly wounded. He stayed in bed for a few days, and just when it looked like he might actually recover, Klinky walked in and shot him dead right there in his bed. That was the start of Klinky's reputation. Years later Klinky started trading between the Arctic and San Francisco. One time he came back from a trading trip north and the authorities hauled him into court for killing that engineer. I guess they didn't have much of a case against him. He just pleaded self-defence and got off.

Henry actually cut his teeth in the Arctic working as a mate aboard Klinky's boat. In *The Big Ship* he even said that Klinky didn't deserve the bad reputation he had. Well, Henry was all alone on that one. Klinky was one bad bastard. It's a matter of record. All kinds of natives disappeared with Klengenberg. He'd take them out on the ice and come back alone. Klinky would cook up some story about the native falling in a tide crack or something like that. He even knocked off a cop. Klinky come into Herschel one time with a big load of goods from San Francisco and the cops

Charlie Klengenberg standing with one of his daughters at his trading post on Wilmot Island.

told him he had to pay duty on it because he was coming from the States. Klinky refused to pay a dime. There was quite a rhubarb, with Klinky arguing that he had to get supplies to his family in Victoria Land or else they'd starve. So the Mounties made a deal with him. They let him go after he promised to unload only the supplies his family needed. They sent this Constable McDonald along to make sure he didn't do any trading. Well, lo and behold, Klinky comes back to Herschel a few months later and there's no McDonald. Klinky said that McDonald had fallen overboard. Everyone figured Klinky knocked McDonald off, but they couldn't prove it. Henry was actually on that trip and he'd get pretty excited if you brought it up. I can see why. It wouldn't look too good on your Mounted Police record if it came out you were witness to an unreported murder.

He had a lotta guts, Klinky did. You'd think that with a reputation like his he would steer clear of cops, but he treated us like long lost friends in Vancouver. He always came aboard the *Roch* dressed like a real gentleman and he'd start talking about some prostitute named Zoe that he was involved with. He died suspiciously later on, and we figured that this Zoe probably knocked him off.

For such a bad bastard Klinky sure had nice kids. He had four of them with a native wife he met up on Wilmot Island. I knew two of them, Patsy and Etna. Both of them were schooled down south and then went up and started a post on Wilmot Island.

Old Klinky was a hard-headed Dane, but the mother was a native and I guess the kids must've got more of her blood than his. Patsy, one of his sons, was a hell of a nice guy. He'd been one of the support people for the Canadian Arctic Expedition of 1913–18.[10] I always stopped in to see him on Wilmot Island

---

10. The government-funded Canadian Arctic Expedition was intended to explore and map the Arctic islands to assert Canadian sovereignty in the region. The exploration leader, Vilhjalmur Stefansson, discovered four major islands and mapped the continental shelf extending around the Arctic while adapting himself to the Inuit way of life, surviving on seal, caribou and muskox rather than supplies.

A young Patsy Klengenberg.

when I went by. One time I was in there and Patsy, good-hearted bugger that he was, had an old Inuit living with him who'd been somehow blinded in both eyes by a single arrow. Patsy took care of that guy for some time. My last time there was in the winter and Patsy said he had something to show me. We walked outside to a shed he had and he lifted up a tarp. Underneath was this blind guy. He'd put a 30/30 in his mouth and pulled the trigger. There was nothing from his ears up. His scalp hung down over his ears. I forget the guy's name, but I guess he figured he was too much of a burden.

Later, when I was on shore posting in Cambridge Bay, Patsy always came to visit me. He had a boat called the *Polar Bear* that he'd anchor out in the bay. One time I rowed out to have coffee with him. There was a couple seagulls swimming about fifty yards away from the boat. I used to recycle the buggers whenever I could because they'd eat the heads off the fish we caught in nets. We were out on the deck drinking coffee and I said, "If I had a rifle with me, I'd knock those buggers off right quick." Patsy went below and he came up with a 65 Manlicher that had two triggers. He put one shot in the air, just to get the gulls flying away, and then picked them both right out of the air—just a cloud of feathers came up. He was one hell of a shot. The year after I left the Arctic his boat caught on fire and the poor bugger died trying to swim ashore.

His sister Etna married an Alaskan Inuit by the name of Ikey Bolt.[11] They spent a lot of time down in Vancouver where old Klinky was. Now, up in the Arctic it's nothing to show up at someone's tent or snowhouse and drop in for tea. That was just a common thing up there even among strangers. When Ikey Bolt came down south he'd walk up to people's doorsteps in North

---

11. Ikey had originally travelled west from Alaska with the Canadian Arctic Expedition. He and Etna ran a trading post on Victoria Island from 1920 to 1932 before moving to Coppermine in the '40s where Ikey became a caretaker and interpreter for the first government school in the area. Etna was a talented seamstress whose patterns influenced the entire Coronation Gulf area. Ikey died in 1981 and Etna in 1987.

Charlie Klengenberg's daughter Etna. Her designs heavily influenced clothing patterns in the Western Arctic.

Vancouver, knock on the door and say, "Hi, I'm Ikey Bolt and I come to visit." One time he was in the Cave Supper Club, a real hot spot in Vancouver, and he stood up and started doing an Inuit dance. Some asshole yells, "Sit down you goddamn Siwash." Ikey came back to the table grinning. "That guy thought I was a Siwash." He took it as a compliment. Etna and him always ended up back in the Arctic. Last I heard, she was thinking of running to be a Member of Parliament.

10

HUNG UP ON A HAWSER

Baillie Island was the kind of hopeless settlement you'd only see in the Arctic. The island was just a few feet above sea level and the whole thing was slowly washing into the sea. Yet for some goddamn reason they decided to build a police post there. They had to abandon it in 1935 and move the whole settlement to Tuktoyaktuk. We made a quick stop there just to drop off supplies and then kept on going. We really had to move, you see, because all the posts were anywhere between 250 and 400 miles apart and you never knew for sure when the straits were gonna freeze up again.

Our next stop was Bernard Harbour. We had another post there. About a day before Bernard we spotted the *Nigalik* up on the rocks. She was a trade schooner for the Canalaska Company and was heading to Herschel after a winter in Cambridge Bay, so she had a full cargo of fox furs worth somewhere around a quarter of a million bucks. It's hard to believe, but she'd been sitting up on that reef for ten goddamn days. It was just a stroke of luck that the weather didn't get rotten and smash her to bits.

The captain of the *Nigalik* was desperate to get pulled off.

He was afraid the *Bay Chimo* would come along. By the laws of salvage at the time, old Cornwall would just have to throw a line on the *Nigalik*, claim salvage on her and the whole bloody cargo would go to the Hudson's Bay Company. We had to hurry, but Henry never was too good under pressure. He tended to get a little overexcited and lose his head. That's what happened down in Vancouver when he punched a hole in the *Old Maid* and that's what happened again when were pulling the *Nigalik*.

Henry tried towing her off with a three-inch hawser but she wouldn't budge, so he backed up to take a run at it and snapped that hawser like it was a shoelace. I guess that got him a little excited because he rang astern, which was a complete lapse in common sense, and we backed right over the tow line. The hawser wrapped round the prop and stopped everything dead. We couldn't move.

We figured it'd be a lot safer fixing the *Roch* in Bernard Harbour just in case a blow came up. We had to anchor there until a trapper by the name of Watson come along in a thirty-five-foot schooner and towed us into the harbour. Boy, was that ever a slow trip. All the while this *Nigalik* captain is worrying about the *Chimo* coming around the corner.

We still didn't know how we'd get this rope off the prop. Dinty Moore stepped forward and said he'd try and cut it off. He'd been a pearl diver down in New Zealand and figured he could hold his breath long enough to free her up. Well, a few of us figured this was straight bullshit but Henry, he was willing to try anything. So Dad Parry gave Moore the biggest knife in the kitchen and he got into one of the lifeboats. Then he put this knife in his mouth and dove in. The water up there never gets too far above freezing. As soon as Moore hit the water he lets out this big scream, drops the bloody knife and scrambles back on the lifeboat. We brought him below in the *Roch* and gave him a shot of rum. Moore was always known to be quite a bullshitter. A couple years later he wanted out of the Arctic, so he wrote to Ottawa saying he had a kink in his guts that took a right angle to his arsehole and stopped any turds from getting out. They pulled him outta there right quick.

Henry wouldn't give up on this idea of diving down and cutting the rope off, so Bob Kells volunteered to go down next. We took a bucket of hard grease we had there and smeared this stuff all over his head and hands, figuring it'd insulate against the cold. Christ, was he a sight. He had no hair at the time because we had to clip it all off to dress that big wound he got in Dutch Harbour. Before he dove in we tied a rope around him just to make sure we got him back.

That grease didn't work worth a damn. He dove in and come up just as quick as Moore. The cold paralyzed him. He could barely move or talk until we warmed him up below with a couple shots of rum.

Henry figured we needed to take a different approach. So we took an ice chisel with a seven-foot handle and added another big handle to it so that it was about fourteen feet long. Then we strung a rope down one side of the *Roch*, round the bottom of the prop and up the other side. We set the chisel over the stern and slid her up and down on this rope so that she'd hit the prop. The water was crystal clear there, so we could see what we were doing underneath. Every now and then a little piece of rope would float to the surface. That kind of gave us a little hope that this was working. It was fifteen goddamn hours before we finally had it licked. Kells went down and fired up the engine and the last of the rope broke off.

We still had the *Nigalik* to worry about. We went back and put a one-inch wire line on her, took a few runs and managed to nudge her off the rocks on the third try. Somehow she managed to get off with barely a nick on her hull and ended up working for a number of years after that.

The whole time we were working at getting the *Nigalik* free I noticed that Anderton was really interested in the operation. Normally Anderton kept completely out of sight while the ship was underway. He refused to go on watch or anything that might have meant he had to lift a finger. But he always got interested whenever there was money involved. What he did was cut some kind of deal with the captain of the *Nigalik* without telling any of the rest of us. He just handed us all thirty bucks and we thought that sounded fair. The year after that I got talking to the captain of the *Nigalik*. He told me that he paid Anderton three thousand bucks. Him and Henry pocketed over fourteen hundred each.

11

GOD ON BOARD

After a short stop in Bernard Harbour to drop a few supplies, we sailed east to Coppermine. At the time Coppermine was the largest detachment east of Herschel Island, so we stuck around for a few days to see how the guys there were getting on. I think it was the second day, we got a report that some white trapper with a shack at the mouth of the Coppermine River had gone nuts. He was threatening to shoot some natives if they came ashore. I was just itching for some real work to do so me and Constable McRae went over to bring this fella—John Brown was his name—in.

Brown's island was about a quarter of a mile long and it was all made up of broken limestone. I brought my rifle along just in case he tried to make good on his threats. We hiked up to a high point and saw a shack on the beach at the south end of the island so we started hiking down to it. The old bugger saw us coming and started walking casually up. He had a long, scraggly beard and probably hadn't washed for months but he seemed completely sane. "We gotta take you in," I said. He didn't see any problem with this at all. He said, "Well, hold on a minute, just gotta go round up me gear." So he went down and rounded all his gear up in a gunny sack and came along with us to Coppermine.

I took John into the bedroom of the Coppermine post and sat watch over him for thirty straight hours. The doctor and one of the preachers in Coppermine wanted Brown to be committed to a mental institution. That meant we had to take him aboard the *Roch* back to Herschel Island, so I couldn't let him out of my sight.

I remember sitting there and seeing two dogs that'd been castrated walk up to a smaller, unneutered dog outside the window. One of these bigger dogs flipped the smaller dog over and the other big one started tearing at his belly. He latched onto his balls and tore at them until the nuts flew out. They castrated this little dog right there and tore his belly all open. I couldn't get out in time to stop them.

John saw this too and started telling me that he'd committed some great wrong in his life, and that he deserved to have his own balls lopped off. He said to me that he wanted me to grab a knife and cut his balls off "so quick-like you can wink your eye." I just ignored the crazy bugger, but he was persistent.

Later old John had to piss, so I took him outside and Anderton was there. I said, "John wants his nuts cut off." There was a big snow knife there and Anderton grabbed the snow knife and said, "Okay I'll whack them off." But John knew Anderton was just joking around, so he didn't keep pursuing the idea with him.

When we got back inside he kept insisting that I should cut off his balls. I didn't pay much attention to him, so finally he said, "Okay, I'll twist them off." I've never seen anything like it. He got his goddamn balls and wound them up until they were just black and shiny, but I guess it was pretty good leather and he couldn't manage to twist them off. I didn't figure he could get them clean off, so I thought I'd just sit and see how far he'd go. I started to get a sense then of why people might say Brown was nuts.

Inspector Alexander Eames walked in when John had about

six twists in his balls. Eames was the Commanding Officer for the whole Western Arctic. He took one look at Brown and said, "White, you make him stop that." So I got him to let go of his balls and Brown said, "That's okay. If I had no balls all I could do with women is play with their titties."

A Roman Catholic preacher walked in about then—John's balls were untwisted by this time—and John jumps right up and starts accusing the preacher of stealing some furs. The priest said, "John, I'm afraid you are mistaken. Go through my pockets if you like." John was off his rocker by this time so he starts rooting around in the preacher's pockets looking for stolen fox furs.

He was a real classic, that Brown. I remember the old fucker would lie in the bed and he'd take a handkerchief and pull it over his face. Then the old son of a bitch would peek out from under this handkerchief to see what I was doing, just like a little kid. I'd look him straight in the eye and he'd pop underneath this handkerchief again.

When the *Roch* was about to get underway to Cambridge Bay I took John down to the boat. There was quite a slop building up. The only way of getting up the boat was a Jacob's ladder— there was no docks or anything at that time. Well, John refused to climb. So Kells swung the boom over the side and I put a rope from it around John's body. Just then a big swell hit the opposite side of the *Roch*. She rolled a bit and John sprang up about four feet in the air. They winched him up on deck and I led him down to the fo'c'sle. The steps down to the fo'c'sle were pretty steep and he fell right ass-over-teakettle, so I picked him up and put him in bed. I rolled into my bunk too, because I hadn't slept in thirty hours. When I woke up he was gone. I was a bit worried, but when I got up on deck it was a nice sunny day and John was laying out there on the deck.

I asked him how he was feeling. "Much better," he said, "but I know you guys are sending me outside and I know I'm just not right in the head. I been in this country thirty-seven years." Then he asked for a razor. I had a straight razor but I wasn't about to give him that in case he tried something, so I found an old safety razor. He shaved off the scraggly beard and cleaned himself up some. I guess that made him feel pretty good because he asked for some work to do. He claimed to be something of a chef, so I sent him down to the galley to work with Dad Parry, and they got along like lost brothers. They were both religious buggers, you see. Dad was always quoting the Bible, and I never ever heard him curse the whole time I was on the *Roch*. And Brown, he was a religious nut. He once got lost in a snowstorm and would've died if a couple Roman Catholic missionaries didn't find him and nurse him back to health. He was fine physically but he was never right in the head after that. He became religious to the point of mania and he started to believe he was God. That's when he started threatening to shoot people. I guess he and Dad found something in common because they got along real well. John just washed dishes and peeled potatoes for Dad.

John acted fairly normal the rest of the way to Cambridge, but Eames was aboard with us and John never did like Eames. One morning he started reaming Eames out. "You're not fit to be in charge anymore," he said. He pointed at Farrar. "This man is in charge now." Then he said he wanted to send a message to God. He went into the wireless office and got Davies to tap out a message. Davies asked him if he wanted to wait for a reply and he said, "No, I'll write my own reply."

A few weeks earlier I'd applied to replace Constable Newt Millen at the Cambridge Bay detachment. All the paperwork was approved, so I got off the *Roch* at Cambridge and never saw what became of John Brown. I heard they shipped him off to an institution in Edmonton.

Years later when I retired and moved out to Pender Harbour, I met a doctor who had been around and liked to trade the odd yarn, Alan Swan. He said he had come across this guy John Brown. He said Brown had been an orphan in Russia and that the great wrong he always talked about happened when he got in a rhubarb with some kid and threw a rock at him. The rock missed the kid and hit a priest in the head. During the First World War he joined up with the Merchant Marines and became a sea captain. According to Swan this Brown character actually moved to Sechelt some years after he was released from the mental institution, and married a woman who was almost as loopy as he was. They both died here right in my own neighbourhood.

12

THE *ROCH* ON THE ROCKS

I was damn eager to get off the *Roch*. She was all right for the other guys but I just couldn't stand sitting around with nothing to do. The only reason I joined the force in the first place was to explore the North, do some trapping and get to know the Inuit. Staying on the boat confined you to the same hundred feet or so all the time. At the posts you had to go on these long patrols with the dogs and that suited me just fine. That's quite an experience. For someone who has never done that to go out and live on the trail and live in snowhouses and have to look after everything that's going on. Today that's just like you were heading out into space or something.

I came ashore from the *Roch* and relieved Constable Millen. There was only one other Mountie there and that was Corporal Belcher. He was in charge of the detachment but he was out of there soon after I came in. Belcher's father at that time was assistant commissioner of the RCMP and made sure his son moved quickly up the ranks. A couple months after I got to Cambridge they made Belcher a sergeant and a week after that they made him an inspector. That didn't bother me too much because I was one of the new guys and never really was angling for promotion, but some of the other guys up there griped. There were some with more than ten years' Arctic service who never made it past the rank of constable. Belcher was honest to me about the whole thing. He told me, "It pays to have your old man at the top of the heap."

Once they'd dropped me off in Cambridge, Henry and the crew headed back to Herschel. Henry had never been as far east as Cambridge before and there were no charts for the area. For the first half hour or so out of Cambridge Henry had the lead line going. When he figured there weren't any more reefs around, he told the crew to put the line away. Five minutes later the *Roch* ran hard onto a reef and stayed there for ten days. We had a little Columbia River fishboat with an Easthope engine at the Cambridge post and we spent a few days ferrying supplies from the *Roch* to the beach, trying to lighten her up. The beach was about a mile away from the boat so this took some time. We tried to make her light enough so she'd get off under her own power, but she couldn't. The Easthope started to act up after a few days so I headed back into Cambridge, about eight miles away. While I was working on the Easthope the *Roch* radioed to say that she'd pulled herself off. I believed that until a trader by the name of L.A. Learmonth pulled in. He'd been helping the

The view of Cambridge Bay from nearby Mount Pelly, 1930s.

The *Roch* hung up on a reef outside Cambridge Bay. The crew is unloading the *Roch*'s supplies on to a small barge in hopes the schooner will sit higher in the water and float off the reef.

The barge dropped off all the contents of the *Roch's* hold on a nearby beach.

Roch and said that actually the *Bay Chimo* had come along and pulled her off the rocks. Henry just didn't want to admit that his old rival Cornwall saved the ship, so he put out a different story.

13

SETTLING IN AN UNSETTLED LAND

The water around Cambridge Bay is full of reefs. It was treacherous bloody water. There was one small reef in particular that hung up a lot of boats over the years, called Simpson Rock. One of the first things I did when I got to Cambridge was put a marker on that rock. There was an old abandoned ship anchored near the post called the *Baymaud*.[12] That was the ship Roald Amundsen tried to get to the North Pole in. He had the idea—it seems crazy now—that he'd get the *Maud* lodged in the ice and just float across the North Pole riding with the pack. He sat in the pack for a number of years but never came close to the North Pole. You should have seen the inside of that ship. She was fitted out with real posh furnishings and a nice wood trim and all the rest. Looked like they were all

---

12. Originally named the *Maud*, it was built for the explorer Roald Amundsen, who hoped to use her to discover the North Pole. The Hudson's Bay Company purchased the ship in 1926, gave her a refit and renamed her the *Baymaud*. The architect of the *St. Roch*, Tom Halliday, supervised the re-fit, and many of the ship's traits later found their way into the design of the *Roch*, including an egg-shaped hull, external ironwood planks to protect the hull against ice, an unfixed rudder that could be lifted through a well in the deck to prevent it from breaking in heavy ice, a large aft cabin and thick crossbeams.

The *Baymaud* grounded in Cambridge Bay. The grand exploring ship served as a source of scrap for the area in its later years.

set to go on a pleasure cruise. She was just barely floating by the time I got to Cambridge, so I went down to her and took off a forty-foot boom, then tied an empty forty-five-gallon oil barrel to one end. I towed it out to Simpson Rock and stood it up there as a warning to ships, and it was there all the time I was in the North. I don't know how long it stayed but I'm sure old Henry got some use out of it.

Belcher didn't waste much time getting down to work. Our first official duty was to set up a fishery in Wellington Bay, about sixty miles from Cambridge. The Easthope in the police boat still wasn't running good, so we borrowed a Canalaska whaleboat to get out there. We took a couple Inuit with us, Sam Carter and Iktow were their names. Iktow was just a kid but he was the only one among us who'd ever been to Wellington before, so we had to rely on him for directions.

The whaleboat clipped along nicely. She had a four-cylinder Redwing motor. I remember that well because halfway through the trip that bloody engine quit and I was the only one on board who knew the first thing about engines. There was quite a breeze blowing offshore and the longer we were stuck out there, the

The *Baymaud* on the beach at low tide.

The deck of the *Baymaud* in 1931.

further we got pushed away from land and out into the middle of Dease Strait.

I'd never seen a Redwing before but she was coughing a bit before she died so I thought something must be plugging the fuel. I lay down in that bloody boat for hours, blowing on fuel lines and cleaning the carburetor—got quite a few mouthfuls of gas. The boat was rocking to beat hell too so I was damn dizzy by the end of it.

It was getting dark when I finally got the engine back running, and by the time we got to Wellington you couldn't see your hand in front of your face, but this Iktow kept insisting he knew where to go. We had that thing going damn near full speed when we hit a sand bar. The boat jumped right over the bar and landed back in deep water, but we lost the rudder.

We had a little canoe aboard so Belcher and Iktow threw it in the water and went off to find this rudder. Me and Sam just sat there in the boat with a lantern to make sure the canoe could find us again. I figured there was no way they'd find that bloody rudder, but Belcher come upon it by chance. He hit it with his paddle after half an hour or so. They brought it back, but we were so damn beat we just anchored and went to sleep.

It was nice and bright when we woke up and we could see that Iktow had done a pretty good job of navigating in the dark. We were only a hundred yards or so from the river we were aiming for.

We haywired the rudder back on and ran up the river a half mile where there was a big camp of fifty natives all out there fishing. I couldn't really see what the hell Belcher meant when he said he planned to set up a fishery, it looked like they had a decent-sized fishery in hand already.

Belcher, Sam and Iktow stayed to fish and I took the boat back to Cambridge. That'd be the first time I was ever really alone with the Inuit. I'd been in Cambridge a month or so, but I spent most of my time just doing whatever Belcher was doing and he never really encouraged talking with the natives. He really looked down on the Inuit. And we had Sam as our interpreter, so I never had any reason to go against Belcher's judgment. I couldn't speak a word of the language, but when I came back from Wellington I saw a few of them fishing for dog feed over on the Ekaluktuk River—that's the river that empties into Cambridge—so I just went over there beside them and started fishing myself. I guess they thought I was okay because they came over for a look whenever I caught one, and I did the same when they caught one.

There were two trading posts at Cambridge, the Canalaska and the Hudson's Bay. Learmonth was the guy in charge of the Bay post and Carson Winsvold ran the Canalaska—both real good guys. Winsvold came in on the *Nigalik* not long after I got back from Wellington, and her hold was right full of supplies she'd picked up at Herschel Island. Winsvold was in a bit of a bind because Cambridge was nearly deserted, everyone was out fishing, and he had nobody to help unload the damn *Nigalik*. So I went down there and offered a hand and we must've unloaded thirty tons worth of coal and oil and trade goods. We carried most of it on our backs off the ship and up an incline to the post.

It was a couple weeks before Belcher came back to Cambridge and when he did he had a different Inuit with him—a fellow by the name of Mahik. Iktow wanted to stay out at Wellington, I guess. I got along well with Mahik right away. I managed to get it through to him that I wanted to learn the language, and every time I saw him after that he'd pick up or point to something and tell me the Inuit word.

In September it starts to get damn cold there and Mahik figured it was about time for me to get a good arthegi. I had one at the time but it wasn't all that great, so Mahik brought me over to his place where his wife Hukonga could get some measurements. She was much older than Mahik, and when I met her she just come up and said hello and then we walked off to the Hudson's Bay post. We got there and she started rifling through

Mahik with his camera-shy wife, Hukonga.

Bill modelling his arthegi, mukluks and caribou-skin pants.

all the skins. Jesus Christ, she went through every skin in the goddamn post. There must've been a few hundred there. She'd pick one up, rub it a bit between her fingers, hold it up to look at the size and then put it back down again. She made a little pile of good ones and went through them a second time before she found a few that she figured were just perfect. We went back to her place and she sat down and started sewing. Sam was there and I asked him, "When does she want to take measurements?"

"She seen enough of you, Bill," he said. "She tell just by looking."

I didn't really know what to think of this, but a few days later Mahik dropped off a pair of mukluks, an arthegi and a pair of pants and they fit just perfect. The boots were made from sealskin, and they kept the water out better than anything you could ever buy in a store. The women used to crimp all the seams with their teeth and then sew them with narrow stitching. You could always tell the ones who made good boots because their teeth were worn half away from chewing sealskin.

The arthegi and pants were made from caribou, and if you looked at the seams you couldn't tell the difference between what old Hukonga did and what a machine can do. That thread never came loose. It was made from sinew taken from a caribou leg. The clothes made out of caribou skin had two layers: you had the soft summer hide on the inside up next to your skin, and a coarser winter hide on the outside. Caribou hair is ideal for winter clothes because it's hollow and doesn't hold any moisture. Sometimes you see them caribou swimming along and their whole body sticks up above the waterline because that hollow hair is so buoyant. The caribou kept you warm but let moisture out so that you didn't get sweat building up inside. She lined wolverine fur around the neck and hood because the ice never sticks to wolverine hair. If it starts to frost up from your breath, you just give it a shake and it's clean again. The entire outfit weighed five pounds and you could sit outside in forty below in that thing and be quite comfortable.

Hukonga's daughter, Howmik, who sewed a tobacco pouch for Bill's mother.

Hukonga and Mahik had a couple little girls, one around four years old and the other around seven when I first met them. The oldest girl, Howmik, took quite a liking to me. Hukonga was just teaching her how to sew, and she'd always bring me some little thing she'd sewn up. One day she got hold of some nice bright calico and sewed it up and brought it, saying it was a tobacco sack for my mother to carry her tobacco in. There was even a little drawstring on the neck of the bag. Well, my mother never saw that thing, but it did hold a fair bit of my own tobacco. That girl was always a little thin for some reason. She could never put on much weight like the rest of them. One year she came down with something—must have been tuberculosis—and she died.

Having a good seamstress for a wife was more desirable than anything else for the Inuit men. Mahik there, he was just a young guy, probably no more than twenty-three, and Hukonga must have been in her upper thirties, but all the younger guys were hot after her. Sam and Mahik actually had a hell of a row over Hukonga.

Hukonga was originally from a group of Inuit who lived on the west side of Victoria Island, and she had been the wife of a real hot-headed bastard there. One Inuit fellow in this group— he was the best hunter in the tribe—had three wives. This was strange because there was a shortage of women all over the Arctic. You often saw one guy with two wives and sometimes two guys with one wife, but this guy was well off, so he had three. Nobody liked him, but he was a great provider for the group. This one young guy without any wife was jealous of the hunter. He wanted a couple wives of his own, so he went up to this bastard who was married to Hukonga and said, "If you shoot the hunter, you can take the young wife and I'll take the other two." And the guy did it, he shot the damn hunter, but ended up being picked up by the Mounties and taken to Herschel Island. He was sentenced to a year of hard labour, which was a joke. He was never locked up at all, and some of the Inuit were a little mad at that. He just joe-boyed around the post, bringing in coal and taking out ashes and slop and things like this. When he was done, the cops told him that if they ever had any more trouble with him they'd hang him for sure. When he went back to Victoria Land the two wives were waiting for him—Hukonga and the young one he got by killing this hunter. For some reason, he got mad at his young wife one day and he hit her in the chest with an axe. It must have been the blunt end because she spit blood for a while and went to bed and finally died a few days later. He knew he'd be tried for murder and hung for sure, so he went to bed. That was something I saw a few times up there. They get depressed or something and they just slide into bed for months or years at a time.

While he lay in this bed, he got after Hukonga to help him hang himself. She wouldn't do it. One day a big bunch of women came over to Hukonga's for some tea and conversation. They all sat down in the tent about six feet away from this guy in bed. He asked Hukonga then, "Could you get a piece of seal line and hang me?" Hukonga wanted to look the obedient wife in front of the other women, so she got a piece of seal line, tied one end to the ridge pole and tied the other end into a loop. He was laying belly down and he just propped himself up with his elbows, brought his head up a little bit and stuck his head in the loop. She tightened the loop around his neck and he leaned forward. She went back to drinking tea with her friends while he hung himself in plain view right beside them. By the time they all finished drinking tea, he was dead. She took him out and buried him herself. Hukonga married Mahik a year or so later, but she remained a hot commodity.

14

PREPARING FOR A TRIP

E verything froze up quick around Cambridge. In early September you had no problem walking on the lakes, and by the end of September, Cambridge Bay was frozen up solid right to the straits. That was a damn scary thing. It meant you couldn't get new supplies for a good nine months. God help you if you forgot to order something, because you'd be without it for damn near a year.

When you were preparing for winter, you were never short of work. The real bitch was cutting blocks of lake ice and bringing them back to the post to melt for fresh water over the winter. You had to cut it when the ice was around six inches thick, or else they were too bloody hard to pack around. You'd cut a two-foot by three-foot piece out, throw it on the sled and bring it back to the post by dog. Now that was tougher than it sounds, because the lake we had to get these blocks from was a few miles from the post. It took days to get enough blocks stacked up. We had a big forty-five-gallon drum inside the post and when the water level went down past halfway you just dropped another block in there.

But we made a real discovery one day. She really froze up

quick my first winter up there and we found that the fresh water pouring outta the river froze right on top of the salt water for a good six inches down. From then on we just cut ice from the river mouth. You could walk over there and get it.

Next thing you had to do was insulate the bloody post. It was small, fourteen feet by twenty feet or so, and there was a partition across one end that split up the two bedrooms. On the opposite end we had a nice-sized coal stove. But there was no doggone insulation in that place whatsoever. You could have that stove red hot and not feel a thing five feet in front of it. All the heat poured out the plywood walls. What we had to do was wait for the first good snow to fly, then we cut big snow blocks and covered the entire post with a blanket of snow about three foot thick. She was just like a big igloo then. We kept openings for the windows and the door and the stovepipe. Over a couple days the heat from the post would melt the snow back a couple inches and it turned to ice. That way you had two inches of dead air space, which is the best insulation you can have.

Starting in November the sun went down and we never saw it

The Mountie post at Cambridge Bay with snow built halfway up its walls for insulation. When there was more snow on the ground, the constables would cover the entire post like an igloo.

again until February. This was when the Inuit really got into gear. They'd be out on traplines for days and days, and Cambridge would be emptied right out for a good part of the time. A guy could get a little lonely if he hung around.

Belcher never liked trapping. He was just completely hopeless on the trail. He was pigeon-toed and knock-kneed and he always downgraded the natives, yet they had to look after him or else he would've starved or died of exposure. Once the cold weather set in, all he wanted to do was play cards, listen to the radio and read books. The books were in short supply—you'd end up reading every book in all of Cambridge at least three times before the trade boats brought in a new set once a year. We got a real kick out of the radio. There was *Amos and Andy* and a few other shows we always tuned in. When it was dark all day like that, we'd pick up signals from all over the world with that radio. We used to set our time by the Big Ben clock in London. The only time reception faded any was when the northern lights came out. Then all you got was bloody static.

There was one announcer we picked up out of Edmonton whose name was Jess Rice. Me and him knocked around together down in Regina when we were both going to college. A few years after we tuned him in up north, he quit radio and started flying planes for one of them bush outfits up there. Quite some years after I got out of the force, there was a group of us drilling in the Yukon. We finished up the job and arranged for a plane to come and pick us up at the mouth of the McQuesten River. We waited out there for ten straight days in the foulest goddamn weather, but that plane didn't come. By this time we were running out of grub, so we started on foot to Dawson City, about a hundred miles away. We only got in there five miles or so and a plane flies over and wiggles its wings at us. It picked us up back at the mouth there and the pilot told us the whole story.

I guess this Jess Rice and another pilot took off at the proper time, but the weather was bad and they couldn't see a damn thing. Jess decided he was going to try and get below the weather, but the clouds went right down to the ground. He dove through the ice in Lake Laberge. They never did find him or his plane.

There were five whites in Cambridge and they'd all come over to the post on a regular basis for the radio or cribbage or poker. Sometimes we didn't bother with the cards and it was just a straight bull session. We got talking about the Depression quite a bit. It was just starting to get rolling down south at the time. The Mounties I run across up there were a pretty thoughtless bunch. Most of them were reactionaries with no sympathy for the unemployed whatsoever. I had three brothers who were really having a bad time of it, so I knew what people were going through and I couldn't bear to listen to these bastards sound off about the poor having only themselves to blame. By that first winter I knew that I didn't have a damn thing in common with most of the other cops up there.

A guy gets a touch of cabin fever if he lingers in one spot too long doing nothing. I spent as much time as I could that fall fishing, so I could stay away from the post. Most of the time I went out with Inuit. Belcher had no interest in it. He was more of an office man than anything. He didn't fit in at all with the Inuit. The Inuit were just clowns, in his book. He had no idea how to build a snowhouse and he sure as hell couldn't handle dogs. I liked the native people. I got along good with them even if I didn't understand their language.

There was a big lake five miles up from the post—caught lots of lake trout and char in that lake. They were big fish too, over sixty pounds in some cases. For lake fishing, we'd string nets under the ice or use spears. Sometimes we went out on the salt water and jigged for cod. We used ice chisels with an eight- or nine-foot pole to punch through the ice. Then you had to scoop all the chunks of ice out of the hole with an old scoop or something.

The women used to come out and fish right alongside the men. Those Inuit shared the labour, and there was sure lots to share. Usually they'd fish with spears, but if they felt ambitious they'd string a net under the ice. Stringing nets was hard work the way the Inuit were doing it because they'd chop a line of holes across the ice and use a stick to poke the net line along from one hole to another. Chopping all those holes in that thick ice took a long time, so I built a little jigger that could crawl along under the ice and string the line out behind it. Once it got across to where you wanted the far end of the net, you cut one hole beside it and fished the line out, then used that to string your net. You ended up only having to chop two holes instead of many.

I'd done some commercial fishing before in Saskatchewan and they all used these jiggers there. It was just a two-by-eight plank with four runners on it just about so long with an iron bar in the centre on a pivot that dropped down about five feet. This connected to a smaller lever that would push against the ice, and you tied a length of three-sixteenths line to the bar. You'd shove your jigger down the hole so's she floated up with the runners against the underside of the ice, then give a reef on the doggone rope. This would pull the bar up and the jigger would shove itself ahead a good six or eight feet. Oh, it just worked like a charm and all these Inuit figured I was some hell of a smart guy. They thought I dreamed it up on the spot and I didn't let on any different.

We had to take the census over the winter. That'd be the reason for my first long trip with the dogs up there. I had to take the census of natives in Cambridge, Perry River and King William Island. It took a hell of a long time just to gather your grub together for those trips. The main thing Mounties ate on the trail was beans. You'd boil up a big batch of beans and then freeze them in flat tins, about half an inch thick. Then you'd take the beans out and put them in little canvas bags. Those beans would be just like a round piece of peanut brittle. I also made big batches of doughnuts out of bread dough. And we always carried a big bag of oatmeal and at least twenty pounds of dried rice for emergencies. Then, where you had room, you threw in some bacon, coffee, tea and maybe some sugar and jam.

You had to check your sled too. That was very important. The runners were made of curved two-by-ten planks that were about fifteen feet long. These planks are flat for about six feet in the centre and then they taper upward about an inch in the back and at the front they'd curve up a lot more. Then you'd put steel shoeing on there and drive nails in just above it so that the heads were sticking out about a half an inch. In the summer you'd spend time gathering up a good supply of black mud and you'd mix this up with caribou hair. You'd take some of this mud, which froze solid by September, thaw it out and plaster it on the runner and around these nail heads. It would be just thick enough to cover the nails. When the mud froze you'd take either a snow knife or a jack plane, a jack plane was best, and plane it off so it was nice and smooth. Once that was done you put the sled together. There were crosspieces connecting the two runners every fourteen inches or so. You just lashed those crosspieces on with a few pieces of one-eighth-inch cod line. It was fairly rigid, but you wanted it to give a bit so the whole sled didn't crack to pieces if you hit a rock or something.

When you're ready to go you get a piece of bearskin and some warm water. You put the warm water in your mouth and then spit it out on the bearskin. Then you rub the bearskin up and down the runner. You just keep doing this until you got a sixteenth of an inch or so of ice on the runner and you're ready to go. One icing would usually last you all day, but if it was warm out you'd have to stop at noon, unpack the sled, flip it over and ice the runners again.

You take a good heavy sled and give it a kick, you'd think it was on ball bearings. It'd slide that easy. But if you hit rough ice and it cracked this mud off, you'd have to thaw some more mud and plaster it back on. The mud wasn't always so easy to come by, so we carried a lot of oatmeal. We had oatmeal porridge for breakfast every morning, but it also came in handy on the sled.

Mahik ices the runnners at midday using boiled water, spit and a piece of bearskin.

You put oatmeal on there and it worked just as good as mud, but you had to keep the dogs away or else they'd chew that oatmeal right off.

When it got warm in the spring, you couldn't hold ice on the runners. You'd ice the sled and it'd pretty quickly melt off. So then you just run on the steel shoeing. It pulled a lot harder than the mud but there wasn't much else you could do.

The last thing I did before we left on the census was practice building snowhouses. They ain't so damn easy to build, but it's a handy thing to know if you get stuck out there, so I spent a couple days and put up half a dozen of them. None were too good, but one managed to stay up the whole winter as the post's outhouse.

When you're building a snowhouse, you have to find the right kind of snow first. It had to be good hard snow. We had this one lead dog up there by the name of Pete. He was a hell of a good dog. That dog knew exactly when to stop at the end of a day. He was just like a factory worker who hears a steam whistle, you know. When he did stop he'd always just lay over on a snowdrift. After a while we found that the snow in these drifts he lay on was perfect hard snow for a house. So as soon as he lay down, we'd push him aside and start cutting blocks.

A close-up of a sled's runners. The light brown patches are where oatmeal had to be substituted for black mud.

To build a snowhouse you take your snow knife and cut blocks about two feet by two feet and about four inches thick. Once you cut out about ten blocks and make a nice ring for the base of the house, there's a trench left behind and you stand in there and cut the rest of the blocks from the inside. You just build it up like a spiral from the inside, and you plane a bit off each side of the blocks with your snow knife so they fit together tight. It doesn't take long for them all to freeze together, and then you go around and patch up any cracks with a little snow. The last block is the key block. You taper that on four sides and it fit into the top.

It took thirty-five snow blocks to make a small house for two or three people. I could make one in about an hour and a half, but Mahik, he was real good, he could make a nine-foot snowhouse in thirty-five minutes. They were warm as hell for about three days, then the snow blocks start to ice up. Snow is a good insulator, but ice is a conductor and the snowhouse would start to really cool down.

In Henry's book he complains about the snowhouse dripping all the time and everything inside getting soaking wet. He talks about how he got stuck having to share one with an Inuit family once and how distasteful it was with all the noise and stink and how he couldn't think of anything as unfit for human habitation as an igloo. Poor old Henry didn't know what he was saying. A snowhouse that's built properly is sloped so the water just runs

Three of the snowhouses Bill constructed in Cambridge Bay for practice before going on his first big dog trip.

Bill peers out the top of the igloo ready to put the crucial "key block" in place.

down the walls. If there was a corner or something dripping, you just shaved it off. Henry also said he improved on a native snowhouse by putting a piece of hide over top. Well, a proper snowhouse didn't need any improving, in fact it would be hard to imagine anything more perfect for that country. It's warm, you can light it with a single seal-oil lamp, it's strong enough to withstand a blizzard and the building materials are free.

A snowhouse is egg-shaped, which is what gives it its strength. One that's built properly will support a man's weight. It seems to defy the laws of gravity. Making the dome come out right was the tricky part but if you cheated and used a piece of hide for a top, the structure would have no strength. The first good gust of wind you'd lose your roof and most likely the whole thing would cave in on you. No, Henry was like most of them up there, they never went out and really learned what Inuit life was all about, but when they got back to civilization people expected them to have all these experiences, so they had to stretch things a little bit. Or else they would take stories they heard from guys who did have the experience and claim it happened to them. I don't think Henry even knew how to make a snowhouse—he never did while I was around.

I was no pro at building snowhouses, but I could build a half-assed decent one. I still got into trouble though. One night I was out by myself and I remember there being a real good blizzard. I went to bed and I woke up with snow blowing in my face. There was a drift of damn snow a few feet deep on top of my sleeping bag. What'd happened was, the blizzard was blowing snow straight at the snowhouse. There was a block or a drift or something just outside the house that deflected all of the snow straight at the wall and it blasted a hole right through until it came in on top of me. It was like sandblasting. I had to get up then and plug the damn hole in the middle of this blizzard.

15

THE CENSUS-TAKER

S am Carter's father was on that famous Lost Patrol. That was a damn shame, and a real bungle—one of the worst for the Mounties aside from the Mad Trapper fiasco.

It was December, 1910, and an inspector by the name of Francis Fitzgerald went off with a couple other Mounties on a patrol from Fort McPherson to Dawson, the same route the Dempster Highway follows now. Sam's dad was their guide. They should have made it to Dawson by February, but they never showed up. A search party went out under Corporal Jack Dempster and they found the patrol—nothing but wasted bodies left.[13] They all died from exposure and starvation.

Their biggest mistake was hiring Sam's dad on as a guide. Sam told me himself that his dad had only been on that trail once and even then he was coming the opposite direction. But another thing is they were travelling the way most whites did up there.

---

13. The members of the Lost Patrol led by Fitzgerald included Constables G.F. Kinney, R.O.H. Taylor and Special Constable Sam Carter (Sr.). Losing their way along the 800-kilometre trip to Dawson, the group, under Carter's guidance, decided to return to Fort McPherson. All four bodies were found within fifty kilometres of their destination.

They'd just fill their sled right full of supplies and hope they had enough grub to keep them going for the whole trip. There were some great travellers in the force, like Dempster or old Sam Steele, but for the most part the RCMP went at it bass-ackwards. They had this formula that you had to pack enough supplies to feed your outfit all the way to where you were going, then all the way back, plus some extra in case of trouble. Well, of course this made for a mountain of stuff, and to carry it all you had to load up a couple of big sleds. To pull the sleds you had to get a whole bunch of dogs, and to feed these dogs you had to pack even more stuff. Now if you miscalculated or hit a snag and run out of grub, you were stuck in the middle of nowhere with a big outfit to support and you were damn lucky to come out alive.

White men had been starving and dying of scurvy in the North since the Franklin expedition in 1845 and never seemed to catch on to the fact this was all unnecessary, because generally the Arctic is lousy with wild food, or was in the old days. All Franklin had to do was take notice of what the Inuit all around him were eating and do the same, and he would have come through fine. But they had this old English idea that there were only certain acceptable foods like venison or fowl. Well, a few hunters can't shoot enough birds to feed a hundred starving men. If they'd hunted seals like the Inuit they would have had enough to eat and the blubber would have cured their scurvy, but they wouldn't touch the stuff.

It should have been so damn obvious because the Inuit were right there with the answer, but the white man in the North was always blinded by his own prejudice. He didn't accept that the natives were people like himself, and that stopped him from seeing that what kept the native healthy would also keep the white man healthy.

The first guy to really call them on it was old Stefansson.[14]

---

14. Vilhjalmur Stefansson (b. 1879 Arnes, Manitoba, d. 1962 Hanover, New Hampshire), Canada's greatest polar explorer, made three Arctic expeditions covering more than 32,000 square km. and discovering the world's last major unknown land masses.

Stefansson was born in Manitoba and grew up on a Prairie ranch just like I did, and he knew how to take care of himself in rough country. He came up with this theory that a white man could travel light and live off the country the way the Inuit did, but the RCMP absolutely refused to give it any credit. When Stefansson showed up at Herschel to start his first expedition in 1908, this same Inspector Fitzgerald tried to stop him because he didn't have enough groceries, according to the RCMP way of thinking. Luckily Stefansson got away and spent five winters out proving his theory and making all sorts of discoveries, while this same guy who tried to tell him how to travel in the North goes out and starves four men to death on the mail run.

Sam must have been a better guide than his dad because we never had any problems out there. I had a rough time getting the Inuit to answer my census questions because I didn't know any of the language. Sam helped out a lot with that. I was learning all the time. There was a trader who used to live in Cambridge and he spoke very good Inuktitut. He'd compiled a sort of dictionary that he left at the post when he went back down south about a year before I got there. There was maybe four hundred or five hundred words in it. His name was Hugh Clarke, and I always took this book around with me everywhere I went.

That was the first census ever taken of the Inuit up there. I had to figure out all their family members and even the number of dogs they had. The Inuit were very cooperative people I found at that time, and I never changed my opinion of them. They'd always do anything they could to help you out.

In Perry River we stayed with an Inuit called Angulalik. He had an old trading post, but he was one of the wealthier guys around, white or Inuit. He had his own schooner and was known as one of the best trappers in the North. Some winters he took in more than a thousand foxes, and that's when the price was around sixty bucks a pelt. You don't need to be an accountant to figure out he made a killing.

Angulalik was one hell of a guy. He took great care of me. I

Angulalik and crew load up his schooner in Cambridge Bay.

stayed there for quite a few days while I took the census around Perry River, and he even came along with me a lot of the time. He told me about a few seal camps out on the Queen Maud Gulf where I could find a few more people to count up. Only thing was, he couldn't tell me exactly where they were because the camps are always moving around out there on the ice. When they run out of seal in one place, they can move twenty or thirty miles in any direction to look for a better spot. It took me three days of wandering around on the ice to find any camps.

I pulled in to the first camp at about eleven in the morning. There were only women and children around because the men were all out on the ice sealing. But it'd been blowing pretty hard for three days and nobody could find any seals, so these families hadn't had anything to eat. I was asking one old girl questions and all of sudden she gets all excited and points out on the ice. "That is so-and-so [naming the hunter] and he has a big seal." All I could see was a black dot more than a mile off. Hell, I couldn't even tell it was a person, never mind who it was and that he was dragging a seal. She rounded up a few people and they started off in the direction of this dot. Sure enough, it was exactly who the old girl said it was, and he was dragging one hell of a big seal. They cut the seal up and next thing you know everyone's walking around with big smiles holding chunks of seal meat. I'm not sure how she figured that out, but then you see quite a few things up there that you can't easily explain.

When I was done with the sealing camps, we went on to Gjoa Haven on King William Island.[15] There were all kinds of natives there that'd just come in to trade. They had a Bay and a Canalaska post there, and I stayed with the guy who ran the Canalaska post. His name was George Porter, but he always liked to emphasize that his name was George *Washington* Porter.

---

15. Roald Amundsen wintered at Gjoa Haven on the trip that made him the first to successfully navigate the Northwest Passage. He named the site after his ship, the *Gjoa*.

He was a half-breed Inuit from Alaska who'd worked as a ranch-hand down in Texas and done a stint in the Marines.[16]

Just before I left, George asked me to take a dog team that belonged to a friend of his back to Cambridge. This friend, Paddy Gibson, had gotten to Cambridge some other way and he wanted his team brought to him. Well, I was all too happy to do that because everyone knew that Paddy had one of the best teams in the North. All nine dogs were brothers. It is always best to have brothers because they've grown up together and don't fight too much and there's no bitch for them to scrap over. Sam had to stay behind, so I got another Inuit, an old fella by the name of Neacoyuk, to bring the police team while I took this damn fine team of Paddy's.

We took a bit of a chance and cut straight across the Queen Maud Gulf, right as the crow flies toward Cambridge. Usually you couldn't do this because there'd be some rough ice out in the middle of the gulf and you'd have to detour around it, but it'd shorten the trip by seventy-five miles or so.

We took one night's rest out on Patoolik Island, a real small island out in the gulf. There was an abandoned trading post out there with quite a history. In the early twenties sometime there was a Siberian Inuit trapper in the region by the name of Mike Herschel. He had a wife by the name of Nellie. She was half Inuit and half Negro. Her father had been in on the whaling ships. At one time everyone called her Coon Nellie but that was eventually shortened to Kunnelle.

Mike was a clever guy. There was a dentist by the name of Miller who came in on a Hudson's Bay boat in '25 to do some

---

16. Born in 1895, George Washington Porter became a trader for the Canalaska Trading Company in 1926 after years of working odd jobs, mainly aboard trading ships. In 1927, he moved to Gjoa Haven. There he managed the Canalaska post before moving to San Francisco five years later. The Hudson's Bay Company purchased Canalaska in 1936 with the specific condition that George Washington Porter be kept on as a trader. Porter returned to Gjoa Haven as the Hudson's Bay post manager, a job he worked at until his retirement in the late 1960s.

Paddy Gibson's dog team staked out in rough ice on the Queen Maud
Sea.

work on Bay traders and trappers and policemen. He had a
treadle machine that you had to pedal to get the dental drill
going, and Mike offered to give him a hand. He would run the
pedal while Miller used the drill, all the while keeping a close
eye on what the dentist was doing. When Miller was finished
all his patients and was getting ready to head back down south,
Mike made an offer on all the dental equipment—ended up buy-
ing the whole set-up for five hundred bucks. He went on to do
quite well. What he did was trade foxes for dental work. He'd
go around drilling any Inuit he could find and always ended up
with a good catch of fox at the end of the season.

Mike was absolutely notorious for making homebrew. In the
winter of '27 he used this old post on Patoolik Island as a kind
of home base for his trapping and he shacked up there with
an Inuit woman and her son and daughter, both around fifteen
years old. Well, late into the winter Mike cooked up a batch of
brew and went on a real drunk. He got into a real row with this
Inuit woman and they somehow managed to leave her son outside and he froze to death. Once he sobered up, Mike felt pretty
bad about this. He felt responsible, so he shot his whole dog

team aside from one small pup. Then he set up a little rack beside his bed to hold the muzzle of his rifle about six inches away from his pillow. He took a couple test shots just to make sure it worked. Then he lay down and pulled the trigger and blew his head completely apart. When I camped there on our way to Cambridge, you could still see pieces of Mike's head clinging to the walls, and two big holes in the wall where he'd taken the test shots.

We took off from Patoolik the next morning and kept aiming straight for Cambridge. We were lucky. We didn't come across any of that rough ice that causes so much trouble. There was quite a number of big chunks of ice, mind you. Some of them stood up more than a hundred feet in the air, but we just went right around them. The biggest problem was the weather. It was getting into April by this time and the sun was shining all bloody day. We had to go back to running on the steel shoeing because we couldn't keep any mud on the bloody runners. It got pretty damn warm out there. We had to travel by night. It was cooler then, so the frost on top of the snow carried the dogs a little better.

Running on steel slowed us down quite a bit, and not more than three days out of Cambridge we ran out of dog feed. That's when this damn bear come up about five hundred yards away. I seen him coming, so I lay down behind the sled. The bear started throwing his head around from side to side. I guess he could smell us. He turned and started ambling away, and I took several shots at him but never touched him.

We had this one little native dog on the police team that I'd picked up in Gjoa Haven. He didn't look like much, but the native I got him from said, "He good bear dog." We had another dog, Jock, that was a real big bugger. We used to use him for breeding all the bitches. All that Jock knew how to do was work and fight. I let both of these dogs loose and they took straight off for the bear.

I unloaded the sled and then took after the bear with Paddy's team. Neacoyuk was there, but I think he had tuberculosis or something by then. He didn't get around very well, so he just stayed back a ways. I think it was a good five or six miles before I saw in the distance the two dogs chasing this bear around. Big Jock, he was off about a hundred yards with his tail straight right down between his legs. But this little native dog, he would run in and nip this bear's heels. Time and again the bear would bring up a big bloody paw and take a swipe and I thought the dog was finished, but that little bugger kept going back for more.

We were coming up to a field of rough ice and I thought if he ever got in there we could never chase him with the sled. The team had seen him by this time and they were straining to catch up. I let another one of the dogs loose and he took off like a shot. He caught up just as the bear had started to chase the native dog. This other dog stopped and stood there, so the bear changed his mind and ran after him instead of the native dog. That dog took just a second too long to turn and run from the bear. That bear hit him in the ass and I bet that dog flew about twenty feet, just like if you took a pumpkin seed and squeezed. Right then the little native dog come in and nailed the bear again and stopped it from killing the other dog. I'd sneaked in close by this time and flopped over on a big cake of ice. I squeezed off one shot and got him in the back of the shoulders, knocked him down. That damn bear got right back up on his hind legs, he was nine foot six inches from his nose to his tail, and started waving his paws around. I nailed him again right between the front paws. That knocked him down for good. I walked up there and he was still jerking a bit, but that didn't seem to bother the little native dog. He was there sitting on the bear's front paw licking the blood that'd come out of the bullet hole. The little bugger had one big claw mark across his ass, just about an eighth of an inch deep. He came real damn close to getting killed by that bear.

That was the only polar bear I ever shot. It wasn't even considered a big one. When I took it back to Cambridge, we stretched the hide and salted it. Belcher was going out that spring on the

The skin of the only polar bear Bill ever shot. It measured nine feet, six inches from head to tail.

Nigalik and he really wanted to take a bearskin with him. I didn't have any use for the bloody thing, so I gave it to him. He probably spent the rest of his years reciting some bullshit story of how he killed this goddamn bear.

It's awful hard to say, but I think where we took the census there was about 750 people or so. That was Bathurst Inlet to Cambridge Bay to Gjoa Haven to Back's River—all over. The Inuit took the bloodline of their mother. So if they were a half-breed they'd be written down as whatever group their mother belonged to.

That was more than seven hundred miles worth of sledding we did on the census trip, and I really caught on to the routine. First, you'd find your stiff snow and build your snowhouse. Then you pulled off your arthegi outside and took a snowbeater to it. If you didn't beat all the loose snow off, it'd melt and your arthegi would be all damp in the morning. As soon as you stepped outside she'd freeze up solid. When you took the arthegi off you were naked from the waste up. If it was minus thirty out there, you didn't stand around too long admiring the scenery.

Once you crawled through the little doorway of the snowhouse and moved all the gear inside, you found a big snow-block to seal the door off from the cold. Inside you had two little Primus stoves. You'd use one to melt snow for coffee and water, and the other to thaw the grub out, maybe fry up some bacon. When the bacon was fried you'd throw in the beans. When the beans were hot, you threw the bacon back in just to warm it up again and that was what Mounties lived off out on the trail.

I always carried an old wool undershirt with me. When you're outside you don't wear any clothing except skins, but when I was inside I'd put on this undershirt and sit there quite comfortable. When you went to bed all the stoves and everything were turned off. We were issued brand new eiderdown bags when we first went up, but they couldn't hold a candle to the native bags. After about a week these eiderdown things would freeze up on you. You'd go to unroll them at night and they just "crack, crack, crack." They'd be frozen solid. When you did get it stretched out the wool lining was frozen together. You'd have to kick it a few dozen times. The natives used caribou skin bags and I picked one up before too long. Shit, it could be blowing a wind chill of minus sixty and you'd lay with no clothes on in one of those caribou bags and be warm as hell.

It's hard to explain all the feelings and the smells and stuff associated with being inside the snowhouse. I just remember it so goddamn good. There's the smell of a Primus stove and the skin and the steam and the sound of those dogs. You'd pull the door in behind you to seal it up for the night and those dogs would just howl and howl and howl. Jesus, you'd be tired and that howling would keep you up all night sometimes. At any time during the night a dog would get the notion to howl. You'd yell at him and he'd stop. Then you'd just be getting to sleep and "whooooooo," it'd wake you right back up again. I've had to go out and take a dog whip and give them a real working over— that'd shut them up. A fella hates to get out of his bag and crawl outside bollock-naked, but I couldn't stand the howling.

Some of the Inuit didn't like the howling either. Up at Wellington Bay one year I stayed for a week or so in a house with an Inuit family. We'd go to bed and the dogs would start up. I could get to sleep eventually, but there was one old girl in there who couldn't stand it. She'd just yell and scream and curse at those dogs if she heard them at all. Most nights she did a way more howling than the dogs. She barely slept a wink and neither did I. No one else in that house seemed to mind. You could hear them snoring and farting away. Yes, it could really sound and smell something terrible in there.

16

SEALING AND TRAPPING

The census was my only real assignment for the entire winter. The only other thing we had to do was take the mail to the *St. Roch* in Tree River, and Belcher did that some time in September. We had a lot of free time, so I put out a trapline.

We weren't supposed to trap but a few of us did. The area around Cambridge was deemed to be some kind of game reserve. Some bureaucrat in Ottawa determined it off-limits to trappers, but people would shut their eyes to it because they knew a guy had to do something or else he'd get bloody cabin fever, and I wasn't about to give up on the whole reason I came up to the Arctic in the first place. It was a goddamn good thing we could do that too. A guy could go stir-crazy sitting in the post.

I just had a walking line, I didn't need the dogs. I guess I had two lines and about seventy-five traps altogether. They were only ten or twelve miles long. Twice a week I'd go around in snowshoes checking and resetting them. That first year I only got thirty or forty. But I had a real bonanza two years later—I snagged two hundred foxes that year. They were worth about $17.50 at the time, so I only made around $3,500, but other

A white fox caught in one of Bill's traps.

years the price was as high as sixty-five bucks per fox. My salary was only seven hundred bucks a year, so the trapping made quite a difference. This is during the Depression, don't forget. When I finally headed south, I had a little more than ten grand.

One other thing about Belcher, he really didn't give a damn what I did. That suited me just fine. It meant I could go out and do what I bloody well pleased. In the spring of '31 I went out on my first few sealing trips with Mahik. Mostly we just hunted the seal for dog feed, but we ate some too. I never really acquired a taste for seal meat. The livers were fine though. In my opinion seal's liver is better than calf's liver.

Out sealing is where I really learned how to travel on the ice. I brought along the usual supply of beans and bacon and oatmeal, but we would've been fine without it. There was always enough to eat out on the ice, between fish and seals and caribou and bears.

For the first few weeks of sealing we had Sam Carter and Hukonga along. This Sam already had a wife, but she was a young one—not much good for sewing. He wanted Hukonga and he didn't hide it either. He was supposed to be out there sealing with Mahik and me, but he spent most of his time in the tent with Hukonga. Damn handy with the women, that Sam was. He changed wives and women just as regular as you change your shirt. Normally, taking turns with another man's wife wasn't too big a deal with the Inuit, but Sam was really starting to push his luck. He spent days and days with Hukonga and didn't help out with the hunt at all. Mahik started to get a little pissed at all this, so I sent Sam back to Cambridge.

We went out sealing to a place called Apiguok. The name meant "sharp," and it was the right name for the place. There were cliffs that went straight up three hundred feet. In the morning Mahik would wash the dishes and hitch up the dogs while I took the telescope up to a high point to spot seals. I'd generally see about five of them hanging around their holes. They had to keep their holes open all year long or else they'd get trapped.

A dead Hudson's seal—one of Bill's first.

When they come up they have a thin roof of ice that's usually covered over with snow. The Inuit calls this an "agloo." The sun would melt the top off these agloos and you'd see the seal just laying there. The heat from the seal's body made the ice as smooth as glass.

There were a number of ways you could kill seal, but we mostly just used the rifles and shot them from a distance when they were pulled out on top of the ice. Henry says in *The Big Ship* that the main way of hunting seal was to put a thin rod with a floater on one end in a seal hole. When the seal came by the hole for a breath of air this rod would rise up in the air and the hunter would plunge his spear or harpoon in the hole. I never seen or heard of such a method, and even if you could figure out how to engineer it, I don't know what'd be the point. When Inuit were harpooning, they used to wait by the hole until they heard the seal expel all his air, then they drive a harpoon into it. The seal will thrash a bit, but he hasn't got any real fight in him because he's got no air. Another stunt was to put a small hole in the ice covering the agloo and then taking one side of a ptarmigan quill and shoving it into the hole until it freezes there. When the seal comes up, the water moves around in the hole so this quill starts to flutter and they know to put the harpoon in. You'd only do that if there ain't many seal around. Another method is they get a four-inch by four-inch block, bore a hole in it, then put some lead in there so it'll sink. Then they take a bunch of spikes and drive them into this wood and then bend them so there's a little hook on there, and then they file them so that they're really sharp. They hang this down in the seal hole and when the seal is coming up it don't bother him, he just bats this block of wood aside. When he comes back down, the hooks catch him and it usually kills him.

This one day I went out and there was quite a ground drift blowing. I walked along for about two miles on this three-hundred-foot high cliff and I couldn't spot a single bloody seal. Mahlk was supposed to come along the bottom with the dog team and meet me, but the cliff was so bloody steep I couldn't find a good place to hike down. He couldn't see me up there either because it was snowing to beat hell. So I started peering over the edge of this cliff trying to find a place where there was no rocks sticking up. After a few minutes I found a spot where it dropped straight down and gradually curved out into a gentle slope. I thought, "Here goes," and I pulled out a knife and notched out a couple handles in the cornice of snow overhanging the cliff. I swung over the cliff holding onto these handles so that I was just hanging off this ledge. Then I let go and spun myself around so that my back was to the cliff. I must have dropped fifty feet at least without touching a thing, just air. After fifty feet I started to feel the snow brushing up against my back and it got heavier and heavier. I was really moving. When I got down to the bottom there was about two feet of soft snow and I plowed into that snow and never even had a jar. It couldn't have been slicker.

When we finally met up, Mahik asked me how I got down and I said, "I just jumped off the cliff." He laughed, he didn't believe me. So we went back to where I slid down and I pointed out the notches up on the cliff and the groove my ass made where I started to touch the snow on the way down. Mahik thought that was the greatest thing he'd ever seen. As soon as we got back to a larger camp, he told everyone he saw.

Mahik was a damn good sealer. He was a real good shot, but he had to get within a hundred yards because he had a cranky old thirty-thirty rifle. Sometimes he'd spend the whole day sneaking up on a seal. A seal has good eyes and a good nose, so it was never very easy to get close to the little buggers. They sit on the ice and sleep for a few seconds, then they pop their heads up and look around, then put it back down and sleep for a few more seconds and keep repeating this. Mahik would lay down on the ice and crawl real slow towards the seal. All the way he'd imitate a seal. He'd raise and lower his head and flap his elbows a bit just like flippers. It looked damn funny, but it was rare to see a seal get away from him.

I had a real nice ought-six and I used to be able to pick seals off at four hundred yards quite regularly. There was a few times we went out that I actually shot more seals than Mahik did. On one trip we shot seventy seals between the two of us. I had thirty-seven and he had thirty-three. Boy, did the other Inuit sure give him a good ribbing when we came back in and I had more seals than he did. They used to tell him, "You should take hunting lessons from this kabloona." Kabloona meant "white guy." We all got a chuckle out of that.

I had a few tricks for sealing, but the best one was a special sled that I rigged up. It was just a small sled with runners about four feet long. I put a mast on it and then hung some white cotton over the whole sled. It looked just like a big snow block, so I could get pretty close to the seal without them seeing me. I also had bearskin runners on it so it didn't make any noise.

You had to kill the seal stone dead. If there was any life left in them, they'd flip over and slide back down into their hole. Sometimes the sheer force of the bullet was enough to push them down the holes, especially in the spring. In the fall they had all kinds of fat on them and they'd just float like a balloon when you killed them, but by spring they were skinny and would sink like stones.

By golly, one time we were out there and I heard Mahik shoot something about a mile away, and didn't think much of it until a few minutes later I saw him up on a big cake of ice waving at me. I went over there and he said, "I shot a seal and he slid down the hole about six or seven feet and he's stuck in there."

We had no means of fishing him out. "Whaddya want me to do about it?" I said.

Mahik said he was going to take off all his clothes and lay down in the hole just like the seal would've done. Then I was to take him by the feet and shove him head first down the hole so he could grab the seal. He said, "When I get the seal I'll kick my feet and you pull me back up." So he went down in this hole, bollock-naked, and he kicked his feet, and I pulled him up. By God, he had the bloody seal. We just laughed. I told a lot of people this story and they all figured it was bullshit.

A seal hole is about the size of an oil drum and the sides are real slippery. When Mahik went down there he had no way of turning around, there's nothing to grab onto. That's why it was a two-man job. Henry borrowed this story from me for his book, only he claimed he did it all by himself. Now that would be quite a stunt. If you went down a seal hole by yourself you'd die there, and you'd look like a real horse's ass when they found you.

I hunted seal with Henry one time. I remember him waiting around a hole about seventy-five yards off. I was there with a rifle too, just a little further away. A seal came up and Henry was taking forever. He just waited and waited and aimed and aimed. I guess he wasn't a great shot. I couldn't take it, so finally I shot the goddamn thing right through the head. Henry didn't like that too much—figured I shouldn't have shot his seal. Well, he would've lost the damn thing otherwise.

17

LIVING AMONG THE INUIT

There's not many places where spring is more appreciated than in the Arctic. After that long winter where it's dark for months on end, the arrival of the sun would fill everybody with piss and vinegar. It'd start by getting a little red in the south, redder each day. We would start talking and betting on when it would actually break over the horizon, usually a few days before it did. Every day we'd gather outside there to see if the thing would show. Finally we'd see just a sliver off to the south and everyone would cheer and hug.

Not long after that you'd get all the fowl coming back. Geese flew in by the thousand. Then you had your salt-water ducks, small birds and ptarmigan. When all the ptarmigan came back in the spring they all went to the same place to breed. There'd be two or three hundred of them all around. They fly pretty strange, straight up at a forty-five-degree angle, then back down again, never in a straight line. I remember one time I had the twenty-two and I got on a nice high knoll where they were breeding. I shot forty-four of them inside of an hour. I gathered them all up and spread them all around Cambridge. Were people ever happy with that! It was the first fresh meat we had all year. I never really

A late spring landscape in Cambridge Bay.

cared for duck or goose, but I had a real taste for their eggs. As soon as spring hit, we'd be out gathering up all kinds of eggs, mostly goose, duck and some gull.

The only bird you really saw year-round was the raven. You could be going along in the dead of winter, minus thirty or forty, and look way up in the air and you'd see a couple of ravens flying around in circles. Now that's something, because unlike a lot of Arctic birds, the raven doesn't have feathers on its legs. It just seems impervious to the cold. What they live on, I don't know. That's one tough bird. Incidentally, raven is the one bird that the Inuit won't eat. They consider it a symbol of bad luck.

All the fresh food made for a real change. It was getting harder and harder to find caribou anywhere in the Arctic, so for much of the winter you just ate the stuff that came in on the supply boats once a year. We had dried potatoes, onions, fruits, berries, beans, rice and peas. We also had canned meat stacked high. There was one type that was absolutely revolting—*Gunn's Beefsteak and Onions*, it said on the label. It sounded good but it tasted just like rags and kerosene. You'd do just about anything for a good piece of fresh meat after a winter of eating that garbage.

Learmonth wearing a head net and gloves. Swarms of blackflies and mosquitoes in the spring made the protective clothing necessary.

Spring had its drawbacks too. Christ, you never seen so many blackflies and mosquitoes. You couldn't go outside without a headnet, and if you didn't have a piece of netting over your bed, you'd never get to sleep. The dogs got it the worst. Their eyes and noses would be right scabbed over with blackfly bites. We smeared pine tar on them to give a little protection.

Belcher left with the *Nigalik* as soon as the ice started to break up. He was in Cambridge for one winter and left the next summer—managed to jump two ranks in the process, mainly by playing a lot of cribbage. Belcher and Carson Winsvold pulled quite a scam as soon as they left. As an employee of Canalaska, Winslow couldn't personally sell furs, he could only buy them for the company. But that winter he managed to corral himself a real nice stash of fox. When they got out of sight on the *Nigalik*, Winslow sold all these furs to Belcher. Nobody knew how many there were, but the hustle was on. When Belcher got into Herschel, he sold all these furs to the Canalaska post there as if he'd spent the winter trapping. There was a lot of talk among the whites about this. Everybody knew Belcher couldn't tell a trap from his asshole, so there was no way he could've legitimately killed all those foxes. Winslow and Belcher both made a nice little pile, but there was no way of proving anything because everyone up there was paid in cash.

I was in on a few rackets myself. I used to peddle off my surplus rations to the trading posts all the time. That was a little more legitimate. They were your rations and you could do what you liked with them. If you didn't sell them or give them away, you'd have to throw them away somehow because we always had more rations than we could possibly use. There was always a huge surplus of flour and coffee and tea and such. The traders were always happy to get it. They traded it to the natives for foxes.

With Belcher gone, I was all alone at the post. I did a lot of fishing over those summer months. The Hudson's Bay post had a good sweep-net. When all the ice was gone from the bay we'd sweep for fish. Sometimes we'd get a thousand in one sweep. We had a little shack on the beach with screens on it to keep the bugs out. Inside there we had racks for hanging up the fish so they'd dry out.

By June of '31 all the natives were off fishing aside from one small family. King-ax-Conna and his wife stayed in a tent right beside the post. He normally went out on the *Nigalik* as a deckhand, but this year Winsvold replaced him with someone else. The snub really depressed King-ax-Conna, so he climbed into bed and didn't get out for three years. That was just like Hukonga's husband who hung himself. It was just something they did now and then. I could never really tell if King-ax-Conna was doing this because his feelings were hurt, or if there was really something physically wrong with the poor bastard.

He finally climbed out of bed after I'd left Cambridge, but Learmonth filled me in on the rest of the story. He started off getting around on his hands and knees, and eventually he got back on his feet, but he needed two canes to get around for the rest of his life. His legs were just like matchsticks.

King-ax-Conna's wife, Tipana I think her name was, had her father living in another tent a few feet away. This old guy was pretty sick, so the family had to draw destitute rations from our post. One day Tipana comes up to me and tells me her old man has died and asks me if I can help her with the body. There was no one else around to give her a hand, so I went into this tent and this old guy was lying there all doubled up with rigor mortis. She insisted we put clothes on him. This meant I had to straighten out all his limbs. I'd heave on them and they'd crack to beat hell, but we eventually got him straightened out, threw some clothes on him and wrapped him up in some sleeping skins. Then I asked Tipana, "Where do you want him buried?" and she leads me nearly a mile away from the post. All the way I've got this old guy slung over my shoulder. She found a rocky knoll she liked and I put him down there, made sure he was covered up nice with another caribou skin that we weighed down with a few rocks. Tipana left an old knife and some tobacco and some cigarette papers and stuff there. Then we walked two or three circles around him and left. The Inuit always used to leave a few things behind for the dead. If the person was a woman, they usually left behind a pot or some pans or something. If the person was a hunter, they'd leave a harpoon or a spear. One time I walked past a grave and there was an almost brand new rifle with ammunition laying right alongside.

I got that little Easthope running again, so about a week after we buried that guy I took off to Wellington Bay, where forty or fifty Inuit had the fish camp set up again. I guess the word had gotten out about Tipana's father, because when I pulled in they all came out to greet me and thank me for burying this fellow. I hadn't given it a second thought, but they figured it was quite something.

That was another bad trip over to Wellington. There was not a single sign of ice when I left Cambridge, but I wasn't more than twenty miles out when I ran into a solid field of small flocs. There was no way to get through it so I went into a little harbour—figured I'd just wait there for the ice to go by. So I was sitting there and I see the wind start to change, then the tide changes and that ice starts heading right for me. I stayed awake three days trying to stop the ice from crushing the boat. I'd get wedged between a couple chunks and they'd pinch the hull you see, so I'd run her back and forth until she was free. She got squeezed pretty bad and took on a good deal of water. I had to have the pumps running the whole time. But the ice finally shifted past and I got on my way.

I had a bad case of the chills when I pulled into Wellington. I'd spent the last three days wet and cold and miserable as all hell. I'd thought ahead and brought a good bottle of overproof rum with me. That was the only medicine we had up there, so once I had my tent all set up, I slugged some back and went to sleep. I woke up a couple hours later worse than I was before, I was just wringing with sweat. I grabbed that bottle of rum and

The Columbia River fishboat pulled up at Wellington Bay.

Mahik wearing a pair of polar bear pants at Wellington Bay. Bill's tent is in the background.

drank a full glass and went right back to sleep. When I woke up a day later, I felt just fine.

I was the only white man in Wellington Bay that summer, and did I ever learn a lot from those Inuit. There was a fair-sized river that emptied into Wellington and we fished all day with spears, gillnets and stone weirs. Every day the routine was the same. We'd fish all morning and afternoon, then we'd split the fish and hang them up on racks. I had the biggest tent there, so at night most of the men there would pack into my tent. We'd get near fifteen in there sometimes, and we'd all drink tea and talk. Those Inuit are some of the world's great tea-drinkers.

Late into the evening they'd go outside to sing and dance. I'll never forget that. They would have a little smoky fire going of willow root and seal blubber. You could see their faces—they were kinda greasy, shining and glistening in the light. And they'd sing away just like a choir. Some would get up and dance and others would sit with caribou-skin drums. The dances re-enacted the hunt. Sometimes the dancer played the hunter, sometimes he'd play the animal. They always ended with the animal dying. I'd just sit there and think, "This sure as hell beats cribbage."

Drying fish at Wellington Bay

Around the fire you could see the women's tattoos really well. It was just some of them that had these tattoos on their foreheads, cheeks, chins or noses. It must have been awful painful. They used to take a needle and thread all covered with soot from seal lamps and stitch it under the skin. When they pulled it through, all the soot stayed under the skin and turned a nice blue colour.

They also played games around the fire. In one of the games they would take a seal bone and tie a piece of string to it, about two feet long. On the other end of the string, they tied a nail. Now, this seal bone had a half dozen or so holes drilled in it that were just a bit bigger than the nail. A hunter would grab the nail and tell everybody the hole he was going for. Then he'd swing this bone around in a circle a few times and drive the nail into whatever hole he was going for. Some of those hunters could go a dozen times or more before they missed. Jesus, I tried that thing one time and couldn't even come close.

They had another game there that I never did try. Two guys would get down on their hands and knees and take a stick about sixteen inches long that was sharpened on both ends. These guys

One morning in Wellington, Bill woke up to find an angry polar bear cub in one of the fish boats.

would be facing each other and they'd tilt their heads back and put the end of this stick on top of their front lip, right in front of the two front teeth. When they had everything set, they'd start pushing. What a show that was! As long as the stick was riding against their teeth, they were okay. But the idea was to get this stick to slide off your opponent's teeth. There was always a little blood when that happened. The stick would go through someone's lip or something.

Sometimes they had a lot riding on those contests. There was one fellow around Cambridge—Kanuchiak was his name, though we all called him Limpy—who I always used to tease about not having a wife. He wasn't what you'd call a catch—had one leg that was a few inches shorter than the other and walked around with a limp. Every time I saw Limpy I'd say, "When you gonna get married?"

He would laugh and say, "I don't know. Sometime."

One morning out at Wellington he wandered into my tent, so, as usual, I said, "When you gonna get married?"

"This afternoon," he says.

"Who the hell you getting married to?"

"Howming," he says, "Anguvik and I are going to pull for her."

I was still new to the language then and I figured I just misunderstood him. Later that afternoon I went out and Anguvik and Kanuchiak are each holding one of Howming's arms and they're pulling in opposite directions. Howming was a pretty good-natured young girl. You'd think having her arms pulled like that would be a little uncomfortable, but she seemed to like being the centre of attention. Anguvik was a big bugger. Quite a few times he pulled Howming right into his tent, but Kanuchiak just wouldn't let go. He'd dig his heels in and pull her right back outside again. They kept on like that all afternoon. I went to bed that night and the bloody pulling was still going on. This Howming, she'd been dragged around so much that she was starting to show a little wear and tear.

When I woke up in the morning, two totally different guys were pulling for Howming and she looked like she was right on the verge of passing out. These two new guys, Avulagok and Koomoya had kept close eyes on the other pulling match. That night, when Anguvik and Kanuchiak got too beat to stand up, these guys came over and stole Howming away to start a whole new pulling match. Both these guys were pretty skookum and neither of them could get any kind of advantage. Eventually they dropped Howming and started going at each other. They grappled around on the ground for a while, tearing each other's clothes off. They were damn near naked when I finally stepped in. I told these buggers to quit their wrestling and asked Howming which of the four guys she liked the most. She pointed to Avulagok. They all seemed quite satisfied by the decision and just went on with the day like nothing had happened. Poor Limpy never did get a wife, that I saw.

I lived in Wellington with them for about three months that summer. That's where I learned most of the language. It didn't take very long. As soon as you learn "What's the word for this" then you start to pick it up pretty quick. The grammar was the worst part. I could get the names of things, but it was making sentences that was always a problem. There wasn't a soul in Wellington Bay who could speak good English, so you had to speak Inuktitut or not bother communicating at all. Most of those people were damn good pantomimes though. They could act out actions to explain anything to you. One old guy there by the name of Katapko was an absolute master of pantomime. He could tell you an entire story and not speak a word. He'd just wave his arms around and make motions like a bear or a seal or whatever it was he was telling you a story about. He'd laugh to beat hell when you tried to put your mouth around some of their syllables.

They have a different relationship with language up there than whites. I remember one time we were on a trip and Mahik asked me "What's the white man's word for 'oglugiak?'" I didn't know what oglugiak meant at the time, so I asked him what the heck it was and he said, "You know, Bill, those little holes in the sky with light coming through." He was talking about the stars. That was just their way of seeing the world. I guess it looks something like that too, doesn't it?

They had no reservations about sex or anything out there— they were much freer than we are down south. We had a canoe out on Wellington Bay that Mahik and I used to fish out of. Mahik sat in the middle and set the nets. I'd sit in the back and paddle. The nets were set across the river. Mahik pulled the net up one side, picked the fish out, dropped them in the boat, straightened the net out, and then threw it over the other side. By the time you finished picking a few nets, you were soaking wet. When we got out of the boat, we usually went in to have a little tea and change our clothes. One time Mahik stripped off bollock-naked and grabbed a pair of pants from his tent. Outside the tent there was a group of women and he started talking to them. He must have talked for a good hour, the whole time holding this pair of pants with his pecker and everything hanging out in the wind. They all just watched him talk. It was as normal as could be.

Another thing they did out in those big camps was share wives. There was nothing abnormal at all about two guys swap-ping wives for a while, or a few wives spending the night with one guy. Often before I went to bed out in camp, Inuit fellows would come up to me and say, "I've got a young wife or a young daughter, if you'd like her to come over and visit you." They'd all offer you the best they had.

During the winter one time, Mahik and I were taking the mail down to the *Roch* at Tree River. There was quite a bliz-zard going, so we pulled into a sealing camp on Wilmot Island. We got stormed in there for three days. The men were all out sealing—there was just women around, and Mahik was damn handy with the ladies. Well, one night a few days later we got to talking in the snowhouse and he told me about all the women back on Wilmot that he'd screwed. He wasn't boasting either.

Bill on far left with a good day's catch at Wellington Bay.

He'd just talk about it like he was paying them a visit. He ran up a good score there, I tell you.

They talked about screwing just like we talk about the weather or something. When we got to the *Roch* on that same mail trip, we put Mahik on the radio. You see, the Inuit had always been skeptical about the radio. They called it the al-out. They thought it was some kind of a gramophone, and they didn't believe that the weekly broadcasts we got were coming all the way from the *Roch*. They didn't know what to think. So just before we left on the mail trip, Mahik asked if he could speak to people in Cambridge on the al-out once we got to Tree River. I told the radio operator in Cambridge at the time, Weston, that when Mahik and I got to Tree River he should get a bunch of the natives in the post to talk to Mahik in their own language. This way it would prove to them what it was. Mahik and I went to see Davies, the radio operator, as soon as we got to the *Roch*, and told him we wanted to put Mahik on. When we first warmed the radio up, we'd always say "*St. Roch* calling, *St. Roch* calling, *St. Roch* calling." Then, "Calling Cambridge Bay, calling Cambridge Bay, calling Cambridge Bay" and so on. The natives didn't know what we were saying but they knew we were repeating ourselves. So Davies handed Mahik the microphone, and Mahik had never seen a microphone in his life. He just kind of looked at it. Then he looked at me and said, "What should I say?"

I said, "Well, you tell them you had a bad trip coming down and it blew to beat hell." It had blown too. It was a bad trip. So he comes on there and says, "It blew to beat hell, it blew to beat hell, it blew to beat hell." He figured he had to repeat every damn word three times.

He stopped then and asked what he should say next. I said he should tell them about all the women he screwed back at Wilmot Island. So he started in and gave a blow-by-blow description about every woman he screwed, repeating everything three times. At the other end the women all nodded and said, "That's Mahik alright!"

People ask me if I ever felt lonesome or uneasy up there. How could I? That was a whole new way of living and thinking and I was always interested in every bit of it. I think going and living with the natives did that for me. Between hunting and fishing and trapping and living, those natives always had something on the go. You were never really bored with them. Christ, if I had to hang around the post all the time, then yes, I would get a little lonely, maybe even a little depressed. A lot of the other Mounties did, but you couldn't talk to them about the Inuit—they just laughed at them.

18

ARCTIC INTRIGUE

Fishing was good that year. We took in four or five tons at Wellington and I brought every damn bit of that back to Cambridge aboard the police boat. I had to make quite a few trips back and forth to get it all. No matter where I was going in that little boat, there was always one or two Inuit who wanted to come along. I had no problem with that. A guy hates to be alone for hours out there on the water. They were a bit of an insurance policy. None of them knew the first thing about gas motors, but if you were stuck out there somewhere you knew the Inuit could stick it out a long time in that country with little more than a rifle and a fishing line.

You had to sit right on top of the engine cover in the middle of the boat so you could steer and run the throttle at the same time. Down beside the cover I used to keep a three-foot steel rod, maybe a quarter-inch in diameter, to check the fuel level. One trip out to Wellington I had several Inuit aboard and decided to play a little trick on them. I lifted my feet off the deck and put one hand around the sparkplug. I didn't get any shock because I wasn't grounded. With the other hand I picked up this steel rod and then asked one of the Inuit to put it off to the side of the boat for me. This guy grabbed the other end of the rod and jumped straight up in the air. He dropped the thing and said, "It bit me."

"What are you talking about?" I said. "The rod can't bite you, it's got no teeth." I asked him to pick the rod back up and hand it to me. He bent over and picked it up very gingerly like he was handling a live grenade. When I grabbed the other end, he jumped back again and said, "It bit me again." All the other Inuit thought this was great. They laughed so damn hard. One by one they all tried picking this rod up and handing it to me, and every time they ended up saying it bit them. They all figured it was something to do with the rod, but they couldn't understand how I could hold it without getting bit. We still had a ways to go, so I put the rod away and tried another trick. I kept one hand on the sparkplug and held out one of my fingers and asked the Inuit nearest me to touch it. Bam, it shocked him again. That threw them for a bit of a loop because now my finger was biting them. They figured I was possessed. Even after we got out of the boat, I could point at one of them and walk forward and they would back right away.

The sunken police boat in Cambridge Bay. One man stands on the stern with a pump. Bill's camera actually went down with the boat, causing a white water mark to appear on this photo.

On the last trip back to Cambridge we put as much fish as we could in her until she barely had any freeboard. We were damn lucky not to hit any rough seas. I had a few Inuit aboard—Mahik and a couple others. Just as we come into Cambridge, we hit a bit of ice. It was just a thin layer built up where there was fresh water from the river. Not realizing how hard even a thin skin of ice can be on a boat, I ran full speed right through it. It was dark when we got to the post, so I figured we'd just turn in for the night and unload the fish in the morning.

When I come out in the morning, the boat was half-sunk. We spent that whole damn day bailing and unloading fish. A five-gallon oil can tipped over when she sunk, so about a third of the fish were spoiled.

We hauled the thing up on land and saw big cuts in the hull where she'd hit the ice. All the constables had to write a daily report while we were up there just to record everything we'd got up to. It was sent on to Ottawa. Mine are probably all sitting somewhere there in some dusty box. I had a hard time justifying all the damage, so I just wrote, "It was found that planking on both sides had been cut through by ice. This condition is not from this one trip alone as there are signs of her having being badly scored previously by ice." I thought I'd get some kind of grief, but I never heard another peep.

The *Roch* came in around then with the *Bay Chimo* not far behind. Whenever the *Chimo* came in it always meant you were going to have a big drunk. It was a damn good thing too. We'd been dry of booze for a few months and were pretty desperate for a drop. The last thing we had to drink come off the old *Maud*. That was around Christmas time. Learmonth and I were talking and he said, "Did you know that old ship's compasses have alcohol in them?" I said no, I didn't, but we both got the same idea. We headed over to the *Maud*. It had one of those big old compasses, so we cracked her open, real careful not to spill any of her contents. Learmonth dipped his finger in first, gave it a taste and just give me a big grin. It was

Bill, Owpulluktuk, Hukonga and Wilson standing outside the Cambridge Mountie post. The constables are wearing arthegis just finished by the two Inuit women.

booze alright. We got three good quarts out and made a few nights of her.

That big drunk when the *Chimo* come in was held at our post. That's where we had most of the big drunks. Sometime around midnight things were really getting going, but the *Chimo's* carpenter was right blotto. He wanted to go back to the *Chimo* so he yelled, "Take me out to the goddamn boat," to Art Wilson, who was the constable the *Roch* had brought in to replace Belcher. So Wilson said, "Okay" and off they went. Well, this ship's carpenter, Chips we called him, was a real ornery Norwegian. We had a little canoe there, about a twelve-foot Peterborough. They got in and started out and this Chips was moving around quite a bit. Wilson said, "Sit still or you'll upset the goddamn thing."

"Ahhh hell," Chips says, "you couldn't upset this goddamn thing." Wilson was kind of a smartass. He dropped the paddle, put a hand on each gunwale and just flipped that thing right upside down. They were only seventy-five feet from shore, so they got in okay, and it improved Chips' temper no end. He sobered right up.

She froze up pretty quick that winter. The weather was calmer than normal and that made for ice like a sheet of glass. I had my old hockey skates with me. Normally the ice was too rough to use them, but not this year. I started skating around there and all the Inuit came out to watch. I managed to get Mahik to try them on and he spent most of the time on his ass. Boy did they laugh at him. Old Katapko come up to me afterwards and says, "We need more of those so we can hunt caribou. We'd catch right up to them."

I headed back out sealing with Mahik as soon as I could. Wilson wasn't interested. He was one of these fellas that goes on the trail and the Inuit just have to look after him like a baby. The Inuit used to call Wilson "Tickyhok," which means "greenhorn." Of course as soon as Wilson came in off the trail, he'd bullshit

Fall scene showing the smooth ice that Bill and Mahik skated on and the Canalaska schooner *Nigalik* at anchor.

Hukonga fishing. The Inuit men and women shared fishing duties.

Sam Carter and Mahik with the post in the background.

with me and anybody else who'd listen about all the silly things that the Inuit had done on the trip. I think guys like him had an inferiority complex. They knew the Inuit was far superior to them in that world, but they'd never admit it.

He was a squeamish bugger, that Wilson. It was a few months after he first come into Cambridge and I think we were playing cards or something in the post. It was in the morning. I remember seeing Sam and Hukonga walking away from her house to the Canalaska post. I didn't think much of it at the time. I guess Sam made a final play on Hukonga. He wanted her for good. Mahik didn't mind it too much when Sam borrowed Hukonga for sewing or something, but he didn't want to lose her. He gave Hukonga an ultimatum, said she had to choose between him and Sam, and if she chose Sam he was gonna shoot himself. Well, Hukonga figured Mahik was bluffing and she went off with Sam. Not long after that I heard a shot. I thought nothing of it because somebody was always taking shots around there. But Sam run in to the post a few minutes later and he said, "Mahik shot himself." Wilson came with me over to Mahik's place, but he refused to go in. Said he didn't want to see that kind of mess. If anybody had a reason to be shook up, it was me. Mahik was the best friend I had up there. We were rarely apart. I went in and Mahik was lying on the floor and he was breathing frothily like he'd been shot through the lungs. There was a hole through his arthegi. I knew there wasn't much you could do for a bullet through the lungs. But looking a little closer I didn't see any sign of blood and I took my knife and ripped his arthegi off. Christ, there was no sign of a bullet hole there, but I seen a little half-moon bruise on his chest. I knew exactly what that was. It was the kind of bruise you get on your shoulder when a rifle recoils. He'd faked it. He'd taken his arthegi off and propped the butt end of a rifle against his chest so he could shoot a hole through the arthegi and put it on again. I found the bullet hole and it was in the floor and run down at a pretty odd angle judging with a pencil.

I yelled to Wilson, "Come on in. It's not too bad." Well, Wilson come in there wincing, ready for some godawful scene. I said, "Watch this and tell me what you think." I propped up Mahik so he was standing, then dropped him. But he didn't collapse. He spun himself around so that he landed on the bed. Wilson and I just started laughing. Mahik said he didn't know how it happened. Said the spirits did it and all this stuff. After that we made damn sure that Sam stayed away from Hukonga. Mahik was a hell of a good guy. I wanted him to stick around. Sam eventually found another woman who was handy with a needle, by the name of Owpulluktuk, and decided to stay away from Hukonga.

Later on that winter was the only time I remember shooting caribou in any great numbers. Most of them had been hunted out by that time, but one day in March of '32 Mahik and I were out there sealing in hard snow, and we spotted a group of caribou crossing the ice heading for land. There were about eight of them. We tried to head them off, but they got ashore before us. We followed them inland for a bit, but we had to leave the dogs behind on the ice because there was all sorts of rocks showing. Mahik and I ran inland a good two or three miles, but we couldn't catch these caribou. I was starting to get worried about the dogs by this time, so I turned back and Mahik kept after the caribou. It was blowing so bloody hard by that time that I had a hell of time finding any tracks. I finally found the dogs after an hour or so and headed back to the tent we were living in. I had something to eat in there and waited for three or four hours. I got worried, so I threw on my clothes and was just getting the dogs hitched up to go looking for Mahik when I saw a tiny speck way up on a big hill. Sure enough, it was Mahik and behind him he was dragging eight caribou tongues. Somehow he shot the whole lot of them. It took us a couple days of dragging back and forth before we got them all out of there.

We were real heroes when we come in with eight caribou. At one time caribou was pretty common around Cambridge,

Lumber and coal left on the beach for the new Mountie post Wilson and White had to build.

but they were really fading by the time I was there. Cambridge never was known for its hunting, and when the rifle came into Cambridge along with the traders in the 1920s, the few caribou herds that were there didn't have much of a chance.

Hukonga was an expert on food. She always knew what parts of an animal you could eat and which ones were poisonous. She knew all the local plants too, and what they were good for. When we brought those eight caribou in she took a few leg bones and froze them. Then she took a hammer to them and smashed them right open. We took out big pieces of marrow about the size of a finger. I considered that a bit of a delicacy, but she told me not to eat too much or else I'd get a "frozen ass." Well, she was right. I ate a few legs worth of marrow and spent a long time after that with my ass hanging out in the cold.

Wilson was a real bullshitter, but he managed to make himself useful from time to time. When he came up on the *Roch* they brought a bunch of lumber for a new post. As soon as the light started to come back Wilson got to work on it. He was a damn good carpenter. When I came back from sealing with Mahik that spring, I helped him finish up the post. That was 1932, and forty years later I heard they were still using that post as a library.

Some of those whites just weren't fit for that country. Wilson at least found things to keep busy. There was a young Hudson's Bay apprentice by the name of Milne who came in the same time

Wilson working on the new Cambridge Bay RCMP detachment.

as Wilson. He was a bit of a smartass bastard too. He came from Scotland and thought he was pretty clever. But nearing the end of his first winter in there, he started to get despondent. He went into a shell and wouldn't talk to anyone. He just sat there staring at the wall. Learmonth told me, "We gotta do something with that guy. He's liable to blow his brains out." We had to work on the bugger. So we started to take him on walks. I'd step into the Hudson's Bay post and say, "Come on Milne. You need to help me with something." After a while I'd convince him to come outside with me and we'd just go for a walk around Cambridge. Gradually he started to talk more and more on these walks until he eventually snapped out of it.

I think that was the same winter that Jimmy Thom was there. He was another one who wasn't made to be up there. Thom was a Hudson's Bay trader and a bit of an upper-crust prick, really liked to put on the dog. He considered every man who took a crack at an Inuit woman just like an animal. He really looked down on any white man who ever invited an Inuit woman over for the night—figured he was above all that.

I went over to the Hudson's Bay post one night. It was just Milne and Thom and I there. We got drinking. Thom opened

Milne relaxing in the Hudson's Bay post.

up some liquor and he got quite right snootered. There was one hell of a blizzard going outside that night. Thom would walk outside now and then for a piss or something. We'd be waiting around inside for him and a couplea times we opened the door and there he'd be laying on the goddamn snowbank with the snow piling up on top of him. One time we dragged him in and he told me that he'd seen an angel. He said that he walked up to this angel and he had brass toes. He really was gowed up. So we'd leave him outside a little longer each time. Jesus, we went out there one time and we looked around and there was no sign of him. I figured he'd just be lying around by the door, but I couldn't see any lumps in the snow. I came back in and said to Milne, "Get your bloody arthegi on, that silly bugger disappeared." I thought he must have walked off into the blizzard. We went out and looked all around and we couldn't find that bugger nowhere. I thought he must've wandered off. He would've been a goner in that weather.

I went down to Katapko's house to get some help. He had two wives, an old one and a young one, and I thought they could all lend a hand looking for Thom. I crawled into Katapko's snowhouse and there, in bed with Katapko's young wife Naniuk,

Bill, right, and Milne practising one method of staving off cabin fever.

was Thom. I didn't give a shit, that was fine. I went back to the Canalaska post and told Milne that I found him and that I was heading back to the police post. Milne said to me, "Goddamn I wish you wouldn't. That bugger Thom—it's hard to say what he's going to do. He's a crazy bugger. I want you here in case something happens." I was tired so I didn't argue. I just went to sleep on Thom's bed.

Later on I heard him come in the door and he still had Naniuk with him. The place was dark as hell. He stumbled to his bedroom and started fumbling around for a match to light a kerosene lamp. While he looked around, Naniuk came and sat down on the bed. I reached out and grabbed her by the elbow—it scared the shit out of her. She got up and ran over to the corner of the room. But it was dark and Thom didn't see this happen. He came over to the bed then and he lay down beside me and put his arm around me. I had a nice beard going then, so I just stuck my whiskers in his face and said, "What the fuck are ya' doin'?" Well shit, it was like an electric shock hit him. He just looked stunned. I got up and lit the lamp. After that he kept his mouth shut on the subject of native woman.

Anderton was another real superior bastard in every way. He spent the winter of '31–'32 in charge of the Aklavik detachment. He really roughhoused the guys there, treated them just like a bloody sergeant major. They were cutting wood for a few weeks that winter and every morning Anderton would line them up outside the post and make them goose-step out to where the wood was. They made it up among themselves to give him the silent treatment. That nearly drove the old bastard around the bend. He'd get lonely and try to get in on their card games or conversation and they'd just keep talking amongst themselves and ignore him. I remember him doing that aboard the *Roch* too. He'd act like an asshole for a few days and then he'd sit down and want to be one of the gang. As soon as you let him in and started treating him as an equal he'd pull rank and start demanding you salute him and bullshit like this.

Anderton was no saint himself. My first year in Cambridge he held back all our tobacco. He was sailing on the *Roch* then and by the time he got to Cambridge, which was the last stop before winter set in, he realized he'd forgot to order any tobacco for himself. Belcher and I had ordered so many pounds of plain-cut tobacco for rolling cigarettes, but Anderton kept our whole order for himself. We had to buy the bloody pipe tobacco from the Hudson's Bay that year for three bucks a pound.

While I was in Cambridge a young German come in, Fritz Schurer. He didn't know nothing and he was just as arrogant as hell. There was another guy there, Pete Brandt, who was a hell of a nice old guy. These two guys teamed up and were going to trap together. They had a little shack, and Schurer got a hold of an Inuit woman and he wanted to bring her in to live in the shack, but old Pete wouldn't have it. Pete said Schurer and the girl should get their own place. That kind of broke the partnership off. I don't know what Schurer was thinking. He couldn't speak a word of Inuit and the girl couldn't speak a word of English. There was no way of them communicating.

Next thing I heard was Patsy Klengenberg brought this Inuit woman of Schurer's down to the *St. Roch* when it was wintering at Tree River around Christmas 1932. She'd shot Schurer— killed him. There was something funny about that because she claimed to have done it because Schurer said he was going to kill old Pete. I don't know how she figured that, they couldn't understand a word each other said.

The way it happened was she picked up a rifle and went outside the snowhouse they were living in and trained this rifle on the doorway. Then she called for Schurer to come outside. He came out backwards on his hands and knees because the door was low and she drilled him in the back right as he was coming out.

They kept her on the *Roch* for the rest of the winter. She was supposed to be in custody, awaiting a summer trial in Aklavik. She stayed in Anderton's bed and the crew all claimed he screwed her the entire winter. When the summer rolled around, Anderton was the one who took her into Aklavik, but there wasn't even a trial held. I guess Anderton went to bat for her and talked to the judge beforehand and, by god, the charges against her were dismissed.

He really lost the respect of everyone up there after that, not that he ever had much to begin with. We used the silent treatment on him all the time. Poked fun at him whenever we could too. He and Farrar went on a little trip one time to Burnside, and they both got lousy down there. They got into the wrong bed or something. Farrar admitted it right away, but Anderton was always trying to hide it. He had to throw away his undershirt on the way back from Burnside because it was bothering him so much. The natives told me about this. They had found it, you see. So I went up to Andy and said, "I was just ashore there and by god if I didn't come across one of your undershirts that was full of lice. It was moving along the ground. I think them lice are trying to get back to Burnside." None of the rest of the crew knew about the lice, but they did after that. Jesus, he was pissed off at me.

19

THE MAD TRAPPER

My second winter was when we first heard reports of this Mad Trapper business.[18] That Newt Millen who I replaced in Cambridge was the guy killed by the Mad Trapper. That must be the biggest goddamn bungle in Mountie history. The way they talk about it now makes it sound like a great piece of police work. When you hear about the Mountie always getting his man, the story of the Mad Trapper is the first thing they bring up. Well, I heard a lot about that story while I was in the Arctic—most of it from guys who were actually involved—and I tell you it was nothing for the force to brag about.

Once Millen finished in Cambridge, they sent him down to Edmonton and then he went on to the detachment at Arctic Red River. There was some complaints coming into the detachment about an Albert Johnson who'd been stealing from other guys' traps. I think Millen was in charge of that post and he sent out a

---

18. The manhunt, which took place in the Yukon between December 26, 1931, and February 17 the next year, was a media sensation all over North America and has been the subject of many books and movies.

couple officers to talk to Johnson. One of those officers was a guy by the name of Al King. We used to call him "Buns" King down in Vancouver. He had a bed right beside mine in the barracks there. I remember him telling me a story about serving in Dawson. Something was wrong with his eyes so he went in to see an old RCMP doctor. The doctor said, "You've been foolin' around with them Indian girls up there haven't you?"

King said, "Yeah, but just once in a while, not like some guys. Why? What the hell's wrong with me?" He was really worried.

"Oh nothing. I was just curious."

That King would screw anything that moved, and he was built for it, too. That goddamn guy was hung like Man O' War.

Anyway, King and another guy went to Johnson's cabin and saw him in there, but they couldn't get him to come out, so they went to Aklavik, got a search warrant and a couple natives, and the four of them went back to this cabin. I guess it was King who went up to knock on the door because he ended up getting shot by Johnson. He didn't die—just grazed his liver. This other constable, MacDowell, was hanging back in the bush a ways and he opened fire on the door while one of the natives, Lazarus, went up to the door and dragged King out of harm's way. They had seventy or eighty miles to go back to Aklavik, but they managed to make it the whole way without stopping, which probably was what saved King.

Inspector Eames was the big wheel up in the Arctic and he worked out of Aklavik.[17] When he heard what happened, he decided to get together a big posse of trappers and Mounties and signalmen. He ordered Millen to come down from Arctic Red to join them. He got nine men altogether, and he stocked them to the gills with ammunition and provisions and something like twenty pounds of dynamite. This all happened right around the

---

17. Alexander Neville Eames was at the time commander of the RCMP's Yukon division at Aklavik. He rose to the position of assistant commissioner before retiring in 1946.

Christmas of '31. We started hearing regular radio news reports in Cambridge in around January.

So they got there, dynamited the cabin and squeezed off seven hundred rounds of ammunition, but that didn't do nothing more than cave in the roof. You see, Johnson was quite a shrewd bastard. He knew this posse was coming, so he turned that cabin of his into a bloody fortress. He dug out the floor and blocked up the windows so they were kind of like turrets. Then he reinforced the walls with sod and extra logs. There was no way of putting a bullet through the place. When the roof came down, a few of the posse walked up to the cabin thinking they might've offed Johnson, but he let a couple shots off at them and they had to turn tail and run away again. This shootout went on for fifteen hours or so, but the posse finally ran out of ammunition and grub, so they had to head back to a base camp they'd set up a few miles away.

They came back to his cabin once they'd restocked and found that Johnson had abandoned the place. A few days later they tracked down Johnson's camp and two constables, Millen and Riddell, went in after him. Johnson was waiting. He tried to shoot Riddell in the head. The bullet just grazed the back of his neck and went through his hood. Well, Riddell was smart— he pretended he was dead. He just pitched forward and rolled down the bank. Millen thought Riddell was dead too. So, like a damn fool, he just turned and charged up to where the shot came from. There was a spruce up there with boughs hanging down. He crouched down and was looking around for Johnson when Johnson shot him. It hit him right around the shoulder and came out between his hips—blew a hole like a water pail in his back. That's the kind of a guy Millen was. He went in head first without thinking.

That night the posse surrounded the camp, but Johnson managed to slip through somehow and he started heading for Alaska. That's when they called in Wop May, the bush pilot, to get some overhead surveillance. May found Johnson's tracks and they managed to catch up to him as he was crossing a river. He dug a hole in the snow and they started shooting into the snow, guessing whereabouts he was. They figured he was pretty near dead, but they kept shooting anyway. Eames was the only Mountie there. The rest of them were all signalmen and trappers. So Eames walked up to where Johnson was and shot him in the head. He swore he'd seen Johnson move, but the only thing that could have made Johnson move by that time was if the fifty pounds of lead that was in him shifted. Eames just wanted to claim he was the one who killed the Mad Trapper. It was a bullshit ending to a bullshit business.

My good god, this guy stood them off for pretty near a month up there. And here they had everything and Johnson, that poor bugger, had nothing. The cops had airplanes and supply teams and men unlimited. He was in this cabin and all they needed to do was take a little more dynamite to this bloody cabin. There was many things they could've done. They could've flown over and dropped a bloody bomb on the place. It was poorly handled. If it was handled right, then Millen wouldn't have been killed.

There was a few headlines in some of the bigger papers when it was all over saying "The Mounties Always Get Their Man" and bullshit like this. Well, if it was only up to the Mounties, they never would've found Johnson. It was the trappers who got him.

20

A BRUSH WITH BAD SPIRITS

L
ater that year we caught wind of another murder. This time
it was near Cambridge, somewhere along Back's River. An
Inuit by the name of Ahigiak had shot and killed another
hunter by the name of Aranuk. We heard about it in the spring
of '32, just as the weather was getting mild enough for the sled
to be useless. We had to wait a few months, October I think it
was, before we could get a team all the way down there.

Wilson wanted to go down and investigate. He got right excited about it, figured he'd step up and get his man like a real
Mountie. I had no complaints. If I had to go all the way to Back's
River to investigate a murder, I knew bloody well that Wilson
wasn't going to take my place out at the fishing camp and we'd
end up relying on the Inuit for dog feed all winter.

Wilson went down there and didn't have any trouble finding
Ahigiak. He was out at a seal camp on the Queen Maud Gulf.
He arrested Ahigiak and brought him back to Cambridge, figuring the job was done and the case was closed. Only thing was,
he didn't bother to find the body of the murdered guy or any
witnesses. The case was still wide open and Wilson was getting
ready to head out on the *Nigalik* in the spring, so there was no

way he could go out on the ice to investigate in the coming winter. Wilson had been in there nearly two full years and I guess he'd had enough of reading the labels on the tin cans. I figured I'd just wrap up the murder case when winter came and I could get a team across the ice.

You always get a little buggy in the spring because you can't really travel. The ice starts to break up and the soft snow makes it hard to walk any long distance. The police boat could only pack so much fuel, so you couldn't head out more than a hundred miles in the straits. Christ, you'd look for anything around the post to keep yourself occupied. When the ice started to break up on the Ekaluktuk River, the main one draining into Cambridge Bay, I said to Learmonth, "I wonder if there's any bloody fish coming down that river." We both figured there was, so we went out to check some fish traps the Inuit had upriver, but we had to cross the thing first. The only free boat was the little Peterborough canoe, the rest of the small boats were all frozen in. That bloody apprentice Milne wanted to come along. There was too much weight in there, so I sat in the stern, Learmonth in the bow and Milne amidships.

We had to paddle upstream for about a hundred feet and then cross over the river and walk up to the traps. There was all kinds of ice chunks running down and Jesus, she was running fast. Had to keep the nose right against the current and then move exactly sideways. Well, I don't know what happened, whether we got hit by a piece of damn ice or not, but she flipped right upside down. I had on rubber boots and they filled with water. Learmonth was a real good swimmer and, by god, he made it to shore. This apprentice was sitting amidships and he started flailing around to beat hell yelling, "I can't swim, I can't swim." He flattened me right from behind. You'd think he was trying to climb on my shoulder. "Grab the canoe for chrissakes," I told him, because, as luck would have it, the canoe was floating right by. So he grabbed it and the silly bugger, rather than just hanging on he tried to climb right up on it and finally he got up

Bill, left, with Sam Carter and Frank Milne on the dock of the Hudson's Bay post in Cambridge Bay, 1932. Courtesy Northwest Territories Archives.

on one end and it kind of held him up. He ended up in a little backeddy with the canoe and they fished him out.

Well, I tried to make the shore, but do you think I could get my feet up? No goddamn way. My boots must've weighed forty pounds apiece with all the water. Fight it as I might, this four- or five-mile current just kept sweeping me downstream. Learmonth was running along the bank saying, "Hurry up, hurry up, you haven't much time," because the bay was still frozen up. If the river swept me down under the ice in the bay, I was finished.

I tried to swim against it, thinking that the current might bring my feet up—no way. So, Jesus, I went sailing right down where the river was rushing under the ice. I made a grab for the ice, but it had been melted to a thin edge and broke off. Just as I was going under I made another grab with both hands out and this time the ice held, but the current swung my feet right up. It was like being caught in a vice. My feet were stuck underneath the ice and my hands were over top so that the edge of the ice was right in my armpits and the water was rushing over top of my head.

Learmonth, he ran out on the ice and risked his life doing it, the ice wasn't very thick. He got a hold of me by the arm and he couldn't even budge me. The current was holding me there. I said, "You pull on my right arm and I'll try to push myself backwards with the other one so I can break over the ice." So that's what I did. I broke over so just my hips and legs were in the water and then he pulled me out. I've never been closer than that.

I gotta laugh now. Old Katapko was not more than a hundred yards from where we tipped over. He was getting a haircut from the barber. He said, "I seen you three kabloona struggling in the water. I'd have gone down and given you a hand, but I was getting a haircut. I was only halfway through." Learmonth and I figured out later why he really didn't want to help us. Katapko was quite a spiritual old bugger. He attributed everything to the spirits, you see. Katapko figured there was bad spirits around the river, so he didn't want any part of it.

Katapko may have been right about them bad spirits. About four days after I fell in, the river cut a channel right out into the bay and the ducks started to come back. There was a young Inuit in a canoe with a twenty-two, shooting all these ducks. He shot one and went over to gather it up. As he leaned over to pick it out of the water, he upset the canoe. He was about two hundred yards from where I nearly went under. The river had slowed down a little then, only about a mile or so an hour. I heard him yelling while I was in the police post so I ran down to the river. There was a little dory pulled up on the beach that was free from the ice. I turned it over and saw that the oars were there so I grabbed this heavy thing and skidded her across the ice about a hundred yards to where the channel was. I got in and started to row. He was drifting down further all the time and I yelled at him and yelled at him. When he got to the edge of the ice he was floating between the ice and the canoe. He should've

L.A. Learmonth, the trader who saved Bill from drowning, standing beside a cairn the two men built atop Mount Pelly.

just hung on to the canoe and waited for me, but he kept trying to crawl out on the ice. I wasn't fifty feet from him when he crawled out and was up on his hands and knees. Then the ice broke. I was there about twenty seconds after he broke through. Never saw a sign of him again.

A total of four Inuit drowned around Cambridge that year. The others all fell in around Wellington Bay during the spring— all widely separated incidents. One fell in the saltchuck, one in the lake and another in the river. We had to take the vital statistics, take note of cause of death, you see. Lots of times we wrote in whatever we wanted—TB or palpitation of the penis or whatever we felt like. So I sent in a report on these four guys, and I said they all died of drowning. Those guys in Ottawa don't use their heads. I got back the snottiest goddamn letter from Vital Statistics saying they noticed the report of these four guys drowning, but that they didn't see any proper investigation into the causes. Well shit, by the time the letter got to me it'd been just about a year since the guys had drowned. There was no bloody way of launching an investigation. In my next report I put the four of them in a boat, sent them out sailing and then tipped the boat and drowned the four of them at once. Ottawa was quite happy with this new intelligence and I never heard another peep.

About a year after that near-drowning, I damn near did it again. It was the spring of '33, and rather than heading out to Wellington I thought I'd check out a river about eighty miles east that I'd heard all kinds of big fish stories about. I can't remember the exact name of that river, but I do remember the Inuit calling it "the river that flows two ways." Mahik, Hukonga, Sam and Owpulluktuk all came with me. We were working our way alongside Melbourne Island when Mahik spotted a couple caribou up on a high hill about a mile away. The caribou liked getting as high up on the hills as they could, where there was a stiff breeze driving all the bugs away. We tied up the boat in a little harbour and the three of us guys went up the hill and shot these two caribou. They were big buggers. By the time we packed all the meat back down the hill it was getting dark. Owpulluktuk was the only one who'd actually been to this river. She just told me to head toward the outline of a cliff off in the distance. The river ran through a high, rocky headland and came out in the gulf at about a forty-five-degree angle, so it was impossible to spot the entrance. Well, I just kept going toward this cliff and eventually we landed squarely in the mouth of the river. Owpulluktuk said there was a good campsite a little ways upriver, so I kept going for a few hundred feet until I saw that we were cruising along at a good clip. I throttled down, then stuck her in neutral, then in reverse, but we kept going to beat hell upriver. I yelled at Mahik to throw the anchor over and it caught just before we hit a big set of rapids. Owpulluktuk turned to me and said, "This river runs both ways. It's running inland at the moment."

We held on there until the tide turned. I got out of there and anchored just outside the mouth. We kept a camp going there for a few weeks, but the fishing wasn't so good so I headed back to Cambridge.

All in all, I can't remember ever having a better time than that spring and summer of '33. I fished, as usual. But for the first time I wasn't all alone in Cambridge. Learmonth stuck around and we spent a lot of evenings playing chess or cribbage. We even went on a canoe trip inland from Cambridge. It was spectacular lake country back there in the summertime. We portaged from lake to lake. It was a hell of a lot easier than it sounds. That country is dead flat and you couldn't walk a hundred paces before you stumbled into a big lake. The sun was shining twenty-four hours a day at the time, so we travelled during the night and slept in the day. That way we missed the mosquitoes and black flies when they were really biting.

One night we were paddling down a large lake around midnight. The sun was shining to the north of us, so it was quite cool. The mosquitoes had come down to the lake in large bunches and the trout were having quite a meal. These big Mackinaw

Owpulluktuk, the woman who introduced Bill to "the river that flows two ways," with Hukonga and Hukonga's youngest daughter.

Weston introduces Hukonga's little girl to one of the dogs.

trout would come up to the surface, open their mouth and plow through a bank of mosquitoes, then slowly submerge. These were damn big fish—some around sixty pounds—and you could see them from a long way off because the water was so clear. We watched these things for a while until I bet Learmonth I could shoot these fish, they were moving so slow. I had a little twenty-two rifle with me, so we gave it a try. He steadied the canoe and I sighted in a big fish coming up to the surface. When it broke water, I shot it right through the head. Its momentum was carrying it upward, so we had a minute to grab it before it started sinking. That was when we were on our way back to Cambridge, so I shot a few more for the dogs. To this day I've never heard of someone fishing with a rifle.

The new constable the *Roch* brought in that summer, Weston, was a bit better than Wilson. He didn't know much about the Arctic, but he seemed willing enough to learn. He did the regular patrols, and as long as he had a good native along with him he was fine. So when it froze up, I left the post to investigate the murder Wilson had started on. I knew I'd be gone for a while.

21

A DOG'S LIFE

You can't just hit the trail after a season of lying around and expect to have any kind of stamina. There's a lot that goes into preparations for a big dog trip. You have to plan out all your supplies, get the dogs in shape, tell everyone where you're going and when you'll be back. I always had a checklist of things I absolutely had to bring. Christ, if you forgot some necessity it wasn't like you could just pick it up at the nearest corner store. You could be weeks from the nearest post.

I was on the trail by myself the one time I forgot something I really needed. One fall the bay had froze up solid but the straits were open about a mile from shore. The weather was horrible, but I was tired of sitting around. So I hitched up the dogs and put a boat on the sled with some grub and I went out about ten miles from the post to the edge of the shore ice. I built a snow-house there and I was planning to get a few seals, but there was a goddamn dirty ground drift blowing. I hunkered down inside and discovered I hadn't brought a goddamn candle. I had no light, and this was in the time of the year when there was only a couple hours of sunlight. I took the lid off the tobacco can and filled it with bacon grease and a rag. That thing smoked to beat hell. Barely put off any light, but it was all I had.

That son of a bitch blew for three days straight—just a goddamn howling blizzard. I couldn't read because of how dim it was so I just stayed in my bag most of the time and tried to go to sleep, but you get slept out after a while. That was three lousy days I spent there. On the fourth day she was still blowing, but the Inuit always said that storms came in three-day cycles. That meant it'd last three, six or nine days. I was counting on three days, so I hitched up the dogs, turned around and went back to the post. Never even took the boat off the sled. It got pretty damn monotonous sitting there. Turned out it was a six-day storm. It was damn near a whiteout on the trip back, but you could always tell the direction you were headed by the shape of the snowdrifts. In the winter the prevailing winds were either northwest or northeast. That meant the snowdrifts always pointed southeast or southwest. A compass didn't work up there, so when she was really blowing, the drifts were the only way of telling what direction you were headed.

The wind was always the biggest thing you had to contend with. It was the difference between a good trip and a bad one. You always hear of the cold temperature up there, but it never got too cold unless you had a wind. I think the coldest weather I seen up there was minus fifty-one. Hell, in northern Saskatchewan one year I was there, it got down to minus seventy-two. So travelling in the Arctic was easy unless there was a twenty- or thirty-mile-an-hour wind added to the mix. The only defence you had against the wind on your face was a thick beard. You'd need four or five months' worth of growth for it to give good insulation. The beard works well because moisture from your breath freezes on there and forms a kind of shield against the wind. I grew a beard every winter, and because of it I never once had a case of frostbite on my face.

Before I took the dogs out, I always made sure to get them in shape. I'd make them run like hell all around Cambridge. These

Bill models the winter beard he grew to prevent frostbite.

You had to exercise the team before setting out on a long trip.

dogs are just like athletes, you know. If they aren't trained up and in good shape, they hurt themselves much easier. They were a rambunctious crew, the dogs I had. Whenever we stopped, I had to take the dogs out of the harness one by one and put a chain on them with a stake on the end. If you didn't stake each dog, then they'd be after each other. You might come out from the snowhouse in the morning and half the damn dogs would be dead. Every single morning, without fail, they'd fight. You'd get the dogs in the harness and you'd have the anchor down and they'd just be lunging and lunging to get going. As soon as you lifted anchor they'd be up and away on a full gallop. Then they'd start growling, growling, growling and all of a sudden one dog would hop over the tow line and nail the dog on the other side of him. They'd get in a big ball with every dog fighting. Jesus, you had to act quick, you had to be in there right away. I used to use the butt end of a whip, and you had to hit them bloody hard because if a dog gets a bite through the foot, he's useless. A three-legged dog can't pull anything. Every morning you knew it was coming. You had your whip ready and as soon as it happened you were in there.

Dogs that belonged to whites were generally more quarrelsome than those belonging to natives. I don't know why that is. As a general rule, a white man's dog was always kept tied up and the native dogs just roamed around. That didn't always work out so good. When I went out to feed the dogs, every damn native dog in town would show up looking for scraps. If you threw your dog a dry fish, one of them would make a rush for it and another one would grab it and it was gone. So you had to stand there with a club, you'd throw a fish down and bang every dog that come near it on the head so one dog could eat. You had to do that with every single dog.

On my way out of Gjoa Haven one time about twenty-five dogs started to follow me. I stopped, and started to yell at the natives to call their dogs back. Some of them did and some didn't. Ended up that there was ten or fifteen dogs following me. Why the stupid bastards didn't call their dogs back, I don't know. All that day I had to take the whip and I'd try and drive these dogs back, but they'd just circle out around me. When I set out they'd trail about fifteen yards behind. You kept all of your feed on the sled and there was no way you could bring it into the snow-house. When I stopped for the night I knew bloody fine that there wouldn't be a bit of feed left in the morning if these dogs were loose out there. So I caught two of them and tied them up.

With the dogs staked and the snowhouses built, everyone on the trail settles in for the night.

The dogs straining to get going in the morning.

That was all I could catch, the rest just circled out around. So I took the rifle and I started to shoot right between their front feet while they were sitting on the snow bank. Jesus, they didn't even flinch. They'd just reach down and start sniffing the bloody snow in front of them. There was only one thing to do. I shot them. All of them. Dead dogs lying all over the jeezly place. I hated to do it. I don't like shooting dogs, but I had no choice. The next day I blocked the two dogs in the snowhouse that I'd tied up. They'd eventually dig out. I met a native later that day and I told him to go look in the snowhouse and make sure the dogs got out. It would've been just the same thing if you were two hundred miles from anywhere and run out of gas.

I had mainly the same lead dog the whole time. To make a leader you just picked a dog that looked smart and intelligent. One of the things you did to train him up was put him right behind the leader. He'd just pick everything up from the other lead dog. We used to say "huk" to get them going. I'm not sure where "mush" came from. I think it had to do with something in the Yukon in the Gold Rush days more than the actual Arctic.

Before you head out on the trail you also have to calculate how much food you'll need. A dog, after a full day's pulling, will eat two or three pounds of feed. When you have eleven dogs and have to worry about your own food too, that's one hell of a lot of food you have to pack. That's why you never missed an opportunity to shoot something.

I shot a few hundred seals in my time up there, but I never

learned to enjoy eating them. Mahik and the other Inuit just loved fresh seal. They'd put the meat in boiling water for about five minutes, just so it would turn a little grey in colour. Some of those natives would eat three or four pounds of the stuff. They'd also make sure to eat the intestines. They chopped the intestines up into six-inch pieces and boiled them up so that they looked like oversized pieces of macaroni.

22

THINGS I CAN'T EXPLAIN

Old Katapko was always on about the spirits. That wasn't uncommon then. There were missionaries up there, and they were making inroads, but I don't think many of those Inuit really took Christianity seriously at the time. I don't blame them. There was a few things I seen in my time up there that I just have to chalk up to the spirits too.

One winter morning I remember bumping into Katapko. He said to me, "I just been down to Burnside last night. Everybody's doing real good down there." Well, Burnside was a good two hundred miles south of Cambridge. There was no way he could go down and come up in a night.

I figured I'd play along. I said, "Whaddya go down there for?"

"Ohh, I just went down to visit."

He went on to tell me the names of all the natives he'd visited, how many foxes they'd trapped and how they were all doing. I wish I had some way of getting down to check the reliability of his story. I asked how he got down there and he said, "I flew there." He actually thought he had been there. Whether it was a dream or not, I don't know.

I know over in Australia the government once investigated thought transmission among the aborigines there and figured there was actually something to it. The medicine men among the Inuit were supposed to be especially good at it. Well, I seen medicine men many, many times, and I never saw anything I couldn't explain. I used to watch old Maneratchik closely. Maneratchik lived in Cambridge and he was supposed to be the top medicine man up there. Mostly he just cooked up home remedies. It mostly consisted of dancing, and fighting spirits. I remember one time he had a real tussle with one spirit. There were a bunch of us in a snowhouse out in Wellington listening to him speak. He went outside the snowhouse and he come back smeared with blood all over his hands and face. I guess he carved this spirit up pretty good. What the old bastard had, I am convinced, was a piece of frozen seal blood cached outside and he'd pick it up and smear it all over his face and such. Guess the spirit didn't have very thick blood.

Katapko always used to be able to tell me exactly when the *Roch* was going to sail in. Making a guess wasn't too hard. You knew as soon as the ice started to break up that the *Roch* would be coming in any time. But Katapko, he would tell you the exact day it'd sail in, and he was always right. Now that doesn't necessarily mean he's got ESP. He could be just an exceptional judge of climate. But there was one time Katapko figured out something that I have no way of explaining. It was winter, and Katapko came in to the post and said, "I think there's a team coming." Well, that was nothing new. There were teams of natives coming and going all the time. He said, "I think it's a white man." Well, that was something. I think there were only two whites in the country, and they were several hundred miles away. Usually if someone was taking off for the winter they'd come in and tell us when they were leaving and when they were coming back. We weren't expecting any white guy back for another two months. I asked Katapko when they were coming and Katapko said, "In three sleeps."

"How do you know that?"

"I feel like that."

Well sure enough, three days later old Pete Brandt pulled in. He wasn't due in for another two months or more. I asked him what natives he'd seen during the winter and he said he hadn't seen a soul since he left Cambridge. Brandt said there was no way Katapko could've known he was coming back to Cambridge. That was the one thing I seen that I couldn't explain no matter how I looked at it.

Patsy Klengenberg, he firmly believed in medicine men. This was a guy who was half Danish and had been down south before and had a bit of education—went to grade three or four. He told me one time he was out on the ice with a bunch of Inuit. They were sealing, but they weren't having much luck. So some of them shoved an old medicine man down a seal hole, right down so he'd be swimming. He came back up twenty minutes later with a seal. Now Patsy was never one to hand you a line, you know. So how the hell can you ever account for that? The only thing I can think of is that the medicine man hypnotized Patsy somehow.

When it came to health care, the medicine men didn't offer much. They made up medicines, but they didn't perform surgeries or anything like that. There were no real doctors around. The traders and Mounties had to do a lot of that kind of stuff themselves. It was basic frontier medicine. Patsy Klengenberg once had to lance a boil off his back with a mirror and a knife on the end of a stick. His wife wouldn't do it so he got her to hold a mirror behind him and he had another mirror in front of him and he cut it that way. He also once stuck a red-hot nail on his tooth when it was bothering him.

I had to perform a few procedures myself. There was one fella in Wellington Bay by the name of Panukut. He had a big sore on the back of his shoulders. That damn sore was as big as a plate and it had eaten down real deep. He made up a cradle of willows and deer hair that he lashed over top of this sore so his

Airplanes brought in supplies—and diseases.

arthegi wouldn't rub against it. It was the damndest thing you ever seen—full of hair and puss and what not. So I started washing it. Everyday I'd wash it. I forget what I put on it, zinc oxide or some damn thing. The doggone thing started to heal up. I had no idea what it was, but you could see it starting to turn grey and new skin moving over it. The biggest thing was keeping it clean. He came down to the post one day with his wife and said he was going to go back out to trap. I told him, "You go out now and you'll be dead before spring. You won't come back." See, I knew he would stop washing this thing and it'd get all infected again. He just kind of grinned. He didn't come back. He died out there.

Sometimes bringing a real doctor in just made things worse. If anyone came in from the outside, everyone at the post would get a cold—and a damn bad cold too. I was the same after I'd been there a while. We'd never get sick unless a plane or someone from the outside came in. Usually the pilot or whoever came into Cambridge wouldn't have the cold but the rest of us would all catch it. When you're isolated like that, your tolerance for disease goes way down. That was the death blow for a lot of native groups.

The Inuit were a healthy bunch, never really needed doctors. I can't think of one time where an Inuit woman even had difficulty with pregnancy. They brought the kids up in the old way, trained them really quick, you see. When they figured the kid was about to crap they'd take it outside and hold it so the kid's ass was pointing at the ground, then they'd squeal at it and make the most horrible goddamn noise. Guess they were trying to scare the shit out of the kids or something. They thought nothing of it. That was just normal for them. A lot of white guys took an awful dim view of things like that, but they had no right to.

Sometimes I saw the kids being carried in the hood of the arthegi. It could be twenty below and you'd see a little kid popping its head and shoulders out of this hood. He knew enough to curl up back in there when it got too cold. When they built a snowhouse they'd throw the sleeping skins down, and before they had any heat going at all they'd throw the kid down on the sleeping skin. He'd crawl around naked on the skin even though it was damn cold.

Learmonth was the best among us when it came to medical know-how. Whenever something serious happened around Cambridge, they'd go to Learmonth. There was this one Inuit, maybe eighteen or twenty years old, and he burned himself bad. He held a goddamn rocket in his hand and lit it with a match and the sparks went all over. They just come down like a bloody torch, burned through his pants and everything. I remember him and his wife going running to the post to see Learmonth. When I went in there, the wife was holding this guy's pecker up and out of the way while Learmonth bandaged his leg. Guess she had a vested interest in the job being done right.

23

MUSHING AFTER A MURDERER

I n March of '34, I got ready to head out looking for Aranuk's body. A few of the Inuit told me they knew Aranuk and that I might find the body about a hundred miles south of Sherman Inlet. That's a pretty broad area, so there was no way of knowing how long the whole patrol would take. I just threw together as many supplies and as much grub as I could and set off with eleven dogs on a twenty-foot sled. It was a damn good team—the pick of twenty-five or thirty dogs. They weren't very fast at all, but they were big and could go forever without a break.

The first stop I had to make was at Flagstaff Island. That was where Angulalik lived and he knew quite a few of the Inuit involved in the murder. I was hoping he could point me to where they were all staying. The trip from Cambridge to Flagstaff is all over ice. Lots of times you'd be out of sight of land. Flagstaff sat right in the mouth of the Perry River, and the only thing marking it off from the mainland was a big stack of oil barrels. The fourth day out of Cambridge I was expecting to see those barrels, but there was a bad blizzard and you couldn't see a damn thing. After a day or so of doing circles and thinking that I'd completely overshot the island, the blizzard lifted, and right in front of me were those bloody oil barrels. It was just luck. I had no compass there because the magnetic north pole was only a couple hundred miles away. If you wanted to get into trouble, you carried a compass.

I stayed over one night at Angulalik's. He told me roughly where all the seal camps were that I needed to find out on the Queen Maud Gulf. He figured I could find the witnesses if I could find the camps, but the seal camps moved around all the time, so it wasn't a sure bet that I'd find anyone.

I went out and I was looking blindly around for a good three days before I run onto tracks. I caught up to a native by the name of Telapahik who said he was going to a seal camp and would take me there. He was the most dejected person I'd ever seen. He had no sleeping bag, was black with dirt and had mounds of snot always coming out his nose. I just had to laugh at the way he looked sometimes, and he'd laugh along with me. All he had to his name was an old arthegi that had all the fur worn off of it.

We travelled until dark. He finally said that he didn't know where the seal camp was. He said, "They must've run out of seal and moved far away." I asked Telapahik if he knew anything about Aranuk and he said, "Oh yes. I helped bury him." Why the hell didn't I ask him that in the first place?

Telapahik figured he could help me locate the body, but I still needed to find a couple witnesses in the seal camps. The next day we started following these tracks that were scattered all over. There was one set of tracks that was funny. There was a normal-sized footprint and then a square print. We followed these tracks and found a camp, and there was a guy there by the name of Poalokok with a peg leg. That guy was just as active as any other native. In fact, Poalokok was one of the top hunters in that group. His leg fell off just above the knee and the rest of it was made up of a few boards. His stump sat on a piece of round wood about two inches in diameter with caribou hair in between

Poalokok, the one-legged Inuk who got around as easily as any able-bodied man.

for padding. Then he had four boards, one on each side and one in the front and back, that went down and tied on to a four-inch piece of muskox horn that he used for a foot. The whole thing was held on there with thongs he wrapped around his waist. I asked him what'd happened. He said he was a young man out hunting caribou and he broke his leg. The leg froze before he could find help. He said the frozen piece just dropped off after that. "Did you have to cut it free?" I said. "No, it just fell off by itself," he said. I was a bit puzzled by this, but you'll see the same thing with animals in the wild where an injured limb just falls off, so I guess there's no reason it can't happen to a man. When I was on board the *Roch* later that year, I told this story to the crew. Henry repeated it in *The Big Ship*, only he fouled it up. He said that a bloody medicine man cut Poalokok's leg off with a dull knife and seared it in the fire and all that old dime-novel malarkey. He also told it as if he run into Poalokok after I left and got the story direct, which would have been hard because the old fella didn't speak English and Henry didn't speak Inuit.

Some years after I left, Learmonth told me a do-gooder came in and saw Poalokok with his wooden leg. He flew Poalokok out to Edmonton to have an artificial leg made. They made up a customized leg worth a hell of a lot of money, but it bothered him so much when he came back to the Arctic that he threw it out and went back to his old one.

Eventually I found the fellas I wanted in that seal camp. They all told me what happened and exactly where I'd find Aranuk. There was Munhik, Ohocoongwak and Agnelliwak, the murdered man's wife, and I told them all that I'd have to pick them up on my way back through with the body.

I must've visited half a dozen of those seal camps before I found the right guys. You'd pull into a camp there and the women would ask you if there was any sewing you wanted done, if your boots needed chewing or shaping. One night out there on the Queen Maud Sea we built a snowhouse in one of these camps. It was a little larger than normal because I knew what was coming. After a while guys started coming to visit and they crowded in and crowded in and crowded in until there wasn't a bit of space left. The snowhouse door isn't very tall, just enough so you can crawl in. There was one guy lying on his belly in this door and another lying on top of his back. I gave them all tea and tried to talk with them.

It was hard to have a good conversation with the Inuit. All they'd want to talk about was hunting. Someone would say, "Not many foxes this year," and the rest would say, "eeee," that meant yes. They'd make that noise and raise their heads and look up. They'd talk on and on this way—someone makes a statement and the rest all agree. They didn't have much of a sense of humour, it was all serious hunting talk. They never quite caught on when I tried to bring a little humour into the conversation. In that crowded snowhouse they got to talking about caribou. I told them that I went hunting a caribou with only three shells in the gun one time. I missed the first two shots and the last one hit him—didn't kill him, but he was crippled pretty good. So I went chasing the caribou and I could run just as fast as him. Finally I caught up to the caribou and stuck a finger in his ass and yanked him backwards. Complete bullshit story, of course, but they didn't laugh or nothing. One of them said, "It's a wonder he didn't kick you." They all thought it was serious.

Telapahik was a strange one, but he claimed to know exactly where that body was. At night, because he had no sleeping bag, he'd just sit down, take his arms out of the sleeves of his arthegi, fold them up against his chest and go to sleep. After a few days out on the trail, the bugger went snow blind. He didn't have any snow goggles, so I gave him a spare pair, but he was already in quite a bit of pain by then. I'd give him some argerol and tea leaves for his eyes at night. That seemed to help him out some. It took about four days of slow going before he got over it.

We headed up Sherman Inlet almost to the head. In some spots along that inlet the banks rose up to several hundred feet

One of the seal camps where Bill went looking for witnesses to Aranuk's murder.

above the ice at nearly ninety degrees. At one point we spotted a big group of twenty or so caribou up on one of these hills. The grade must have been sixty percent, but they saw us and roared at full speed down this bloody bank. Then they stopped at the bottom to look at us for a while. I had my rifle out of course, hoping they'd get just a little closer. They stared at us for one or two minutes at the bottom of this hill, and then ran at a full gallop right back to the top again. It was one of the damndest things I've ever seen. It was just like they were floating up the side of this hill. So they stood at the top for a bit and then roared back down and then back up again.

We turned off the inlet and went up a river heading south and came up on a big chain of lakes. The country was flat there with hundreds of pingos all over the place. Pingos are little hills made of ice and soil formed by water running into cracks and freezing. When the water freezes, it expands and heaves up the ground in a mound. It can keep heaving up till it's sticking up like a haystack.

There was never any shortage of game there. Holy shit, there was muskox, rabbits, ptarmigan, fox and a few more bands of caribou all over the place. Whenever we needed a little fresh meat, I'd just slouch down in the snow and peg something off. At one point on the trail I remember seeing a fox track, and as I walked on I noticed there was a lemming trail that came in from the side. Eventually they met, and where they met there was a little drop of blood and then just a fox trail heading off. It was a whole story written in the snow.

There was one lake we crossed that was about fifteen miles long and it had several big pressure ridges. Some of these damn ridges were about ten feet high. They're usually made when the ice expands and, because of the pressure, it heaves upwards at its weakest point. They were a real bitch to cross, too. A lot of times there'd be big pools of water all around the ridges, and before you knew it you were walking through water. The ridges made for a rough ride, and you had to keep a pretty keen eye out so that you didn't bust mud off your runners.

I started my own legend while I was crossing that lake with Telapahik. We were crossing those ridges and the sled's speed was just a little faster than a walk, about five miles an hour. If you jogged you could catch up. I'd just walk behind the sled as it would pull away, pull away and get out of sight. But I didn't worry, I'd follow the tracks in the snow. So I got way hell and gone back one time and I started to jog. I guess it took me about three-quarters of an hour before I caught up again. Telapahik wondered what held me up. I said, "I fell into a seal hole." Well, there was no seal holes there, you know. He said, "Yeah, I was wondering what made those pressure ridges. There must be a big seal down there pushing all that ice up." The silly bugger. I wasn't wet or anything. A few weeks later, when we were in Gjoa Haven, I ran into George Porter. He came up to the Hudson's Bay post where I was and says, "There's a new story going around now. Some lake down there has got a seal so big it's pushing up pressure ridges." You were always hearing stories like this, but that was the time I saw one get started. It's probably still going on up there.

Every lake has a big fish up there, you know. They have legends for everything. There was this one lake up there with big char. I caught a fifty-two-pound char there once. Every now and

An Inuit woman tows her child around one of the seal camps on a piece of hide.

then we'd pull the net out and there'd be a big chunk of web gone. The Inuit said, "That's the big fish. He just goes right through the net. Doesn't notice a thing." Ikluktutiak was the name of that lake. It has an English name now. That's a goddamn crime. Some bastard down in Ottawa names it and he's never even seen it. That was just a little inland from Cambridge.

About a hundred miles south of the Adelaide Peninsula we finally came up on this spot where the natives had camped when Aranuk was shot. There was quite a bit of snow on the ground, but we were lucky and found the corpse. Another six feet to the side and he would've been buried under a snowdrift. Just a few bones together with the skull were scattered about, along with a duffle that he'd been wearing when he was shot, containing the bones of his foot. I took a few pictures for evidence and gathered up the skull and the duffle. I needed to get an identification on the body and I was pretty sure they could do it by the teeth in the skull and his wife's sewing on the duffle.

I dropped off Telapahik in Gjoa Haven after that. I gave him an agreed-upon number of foxes and I figured he'd go and buy a bag or a new arthegi or something, but he ended up getting a whole bunch of jewelry for some woman he liked.

It was rough going for the last few days of that trip into Gjoa

Aranuk's remains

Haven. It'd been three weeks since I left Cambridge—quite a bit longer than I'd planned. By the time we got to Gjoa Haven supplies were running short. We were out of kerosene for the Primus stoves and only had a day or so more on the dog feed. But there was no chance of us going hungry. I know a lot of other Mounties, like those ones on the Lost Patrol, would've thought things were pretty desperate, but there was always seal. I never enjoyed seal too much, but the dogs and all the Inuit just loved the stuff.

I stayed in Gjoa Haven for a couple days, just long enough to get more supplies loaded on the sled and give the dogs a bit of a rest. While I was there I saw a real old Inuit smoking a soapstone pipe. I saw that the cap on top of the pipe to protect it from the wind was a piece of nice brass. I asked to take a look at this pipe and then I traded him my crooked-stemmed briar pipe for it. I had no interest in the pipe, but that goddamn piece of brass was a button off the uniform of someone from the Franklin Expedition of 1845. I ended up giving it to a museum.

I went back out on the ice to pick up the witnesses and head back with them to Cambridge. It wasn't too hard to find them this time, so they all hitched up their own teams and followed me. We stopped for one night at Angulalik's, and he told me all

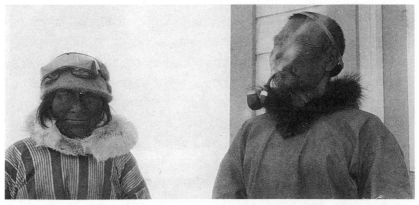

Two Inuit Bill met in Gjoa Haven. On the left is Kabloona, who was Roald Amundsen's seamstress. On the right is the man who was using a button from the 1845 Franklin Expedition as a cap for his tobacco pipe.

the births and all the deaths that'd taken place that winter. He also knew exactly how every Inuit hunter and trapper did for the season. That guy had the best memory of any man I've ever met.

Not more than a day out of Angulalik's place, Agnelliwak's sled overturned and she buggered up her ankle pretty good. She had to ride on the sled for the rest of the trip, slowing us down a little more. On top of that, the weather was starting to get miserable. It was April by this time, so we couldn't keep any ice on the runners and had to kick all the mud off and just run on the steel shoeing. When you're running on the steel, the sled only moves at a medium-paced walk. We were taking longer than I'd hoped again, but with the sleds moving so slow I had lots of time to shoot seal and keep the dogs and the Inuit going with fresh meat.

We got into Cambridge near the end of April, six weeks after I'd left. That whole trip was about a thousand miles if you look at it on a map, but the ice was bad that year. It froze up rougher than usual, so there was a lot of long detours. The trip ended up closer to twelve hundred miles. I figured I'd done pretty good for such a long trip. We didn't lose any dogs or suffer from any really bad accidents. The worst we come across was Agnelliwak's twisted ankle and a bit of minor frostbite. The bloody sunburn was the worst I got. I always thought Arctic sunburn was worse than frostbite. It can be well below zero out there but you can get a wicked sunburn that makes your face crack and peel where you don't have a beard. All the exposed parts of my face were burned as black as coal. I shaved my beard off when I got into Cambridge and it looked like I had a two-tone paint job. All the skin under my beard was pale white, and the rest of it was black.

Ahigiak, the accused murderer, and his wife Hitkogaluk were in Cambridge when we arrived. It'd been a year since Wilson first hauled him in, and in the meantime they'd been out fishing and sealing. We didn't keep Ahigiak in custody or anything, he was free to hunt and trap and fish as long as he eventually came back to Cambridge. That was the way things were up there. Ahigiak didn't have a clue what all the fuss was about, but he was happy to do whatever we said.

Applying white man's law to these old-time Inuit was kind of pointless. Rudolph Johnson told me a story about a couple Inuit who were tried for murder five years before I got up there. These two Inuit, Alikomiak and Tatamanga, had murdered four Inuit because of a row they had over women. A couple cops, Doak and Woolems, hauled them into the post at Tree River, but the post was too small to keep them both, so they let Tatamanga go back out sealing. The deal was he'd come back from sealing in the spring and then they'd head off for a trial in Herschel. Alikomiak had to stay and joe-boy around the post.

One day he spilled a bucket of slops in the post and Doak chewed him out. Alikomiak waited for Doak to lay down in bed and grabbed a rifle and shot the cop right through the hip. The bullet ranged up through his body and killed him. There was a Hudson's Bay trader, Otto Binder, who had a post not far away. He was in the habit of coming over to the police post every morning for coffee. Alikomiak knew this, so he found a nice peephole at one of the windows of the post, waited for Binder to walk into his sights and shot him dead right through the heart.

He took off for a seal camp then but they eventually nabbed him and took him and Tatamanga over to Herschel for a trial. A judge, two lawyers—one prosecuting, one defending—and a hangman were brought into Herschel. With the hangman there, there was never too much doubt about the outcome. Rudolph said it was the funniest thing. This hangman could barely get outside because the dogs just hated him. They sensed something in that guy and just went after him wherever he went, all of them barking and snarling. The two Inuit were found guilty and sentenced to hang a few days after the trial.

The Inuit have an old tradition where dying people actually

pick out their grave sites. These two Inuit got to pick out their graves, but they also had to dig the things out. So they did this, but Herschel Island is mostly permafrost. Every day the sun would beat down and these graves would partly fill up with melt water. These guys were locked up the night before they were going to be hanged and they asked permission to bail the water out of those graves—said they didn't want to lay in that cold water. So the police let them free to bail the graves out.

As they were walking back from bailing, these two Inuit ran into the judge. He runs into the post and yells, "The prisoners have escaped."

There was one constable in there, and he says, "Whaddya mean?"

"I just ran into those prisoners. They've sprung out of jail."

"They haven't escaped, we just haven't bothered locking them up yet."

The old judge could hardly believe it. I guess he was worried these vicious criminals might come after him.

Eventually these two came back to the post. The next morning a constable went to grab them to be hanged and they were both sound asleep. They woke Alikomiak up and hung him. He was light and they had to drop him twice to kill him. They should have put weights on the bugger. It was bloody awful.

They went back to grab Tatamanga, and the bugger had gone back to sleep. Apparently he didn't think getting hung was anything to lose sleep over. The old-time Inuit really didn't think about death the same way we did, and it just made the law seem kind of ridiculous.

Ahigiak fessed up to everything once I'd rounded up all the witnesses. He told me the whole story. Ahigiak said he'd been friends for years with Aranuk. They traded wives whenever they felt like it, just like they all did. He didn't mind that. But he got it in his head that Aranuk was going to steal his wife, and the guy already had two. That would've left Ahigiak without anyone to sew for him. He didn't mind the guy screwing his wife, but he didn't want to be without boots. So he decided to shoot Aranuk. He went to a lot of trouble. He got a target, set it up and told Aranuk he should sight his gun in with this target. Aranuk started shooting at the target laying down in the snow—that's how they always shot. When Aranuk had unloaded his rifle he got up and Ahigiak shot him in the back. He said Aranuk jumped up in the air and turned around looking awful surprised. Then he said, "I shot him in the front and Aranuk fell down and he was dead then." Just as a matter of fact, like he was talking about recycling a hurt dog or something.

We had just enough time to head over to Tree River before the ice broke up—that's where the *Roch* was frozen in for the winter again. When the ice finally freed up, we'd take Ahigiak and the witnesses down in the *Roch* to a trial in Coppermine. That was quite a trip over to Tree River. There was six of us altogether. I got along quite well with Ahigiak. He wasn't a bad guy. I used to hand him my rifle and send him on ahead of us to kill seals. I wasn't afraid of him. Tree River was three hundred miles from Cambridge, but we had no troubles.

She was a full boat on the *Roch*. There was somewhere around fifty dogs and they had a full crew already on board before the six of us rolled in. It'd be two and a half months, late July, when the ice finally broke up enough for us to sail.

In the meantime we had a great time. All the winter work was finished on the *Roch*, so we spent a lot of time hiking around Tree River. By that time Anderton had been replaced by a Sergeant George Makinson. He was sure hot after the dollar, that guy. One day we were hiking inland from Tree River pegging off seals for dog feed. Now, Makinson was a pretty decent shot and he just couldn't pass up the opportunity for a bet, so he said, "I'll bet you twenty-five bucks that I can beat you in a shooting match." I said, "You're on."

I had been playing a fair bit of chess with Learmonth that summer and neither one of us was any good at it. But the fellas in the boat were playing chess as well. Makinson was supposed to be pretty good, so he added to the original bet. He said, "I bet you twenty-five bucks I can beat you at a game of chess as well." He figured he was going to make fifty bucks easy.

We went back down to the *Roch* and the crew was all against Makinson. The crew liked him better than Anderton, but it's hard to root for a commanding officer. He wanted to play two or three practice games before the final showdown, but I wouldn't have it. I wanted to play for money. We sat down and started to play. I still can't figure out how the hell it happened, but within three or four moves I had him checkmated. I think that was the quickest game I ever played. And boy, did the crew ever roast him over that. He didn't pay up for a few days, but he finally did after considerable razzing from the crew.

Next we got onto the shooting match. Makinson wanted us both to use his gun. I said, "No goddamn way. You use your bloody rifle and I'll use mine." Then he said, "We'll shoot from a hundred yards." I said, "We'll shoot from a hundred yards and five hundred yards, that's a real shooting match." He wasn't too keen on the longer shooting. He agreed, but he wanted to have a couple days worth of practice shooting. I said, "Fine. Have your practice."

A couple days after that a few of us were hiking up Tree River. There were some big cliffs there and we noticed a patch of white way up on the cliff, and we were wondering if it was a rabbit or just a patch of snow. I took out my rifle and said, "I'll tell you if that's a rabbit or not." So I shot at it and a puff of white flew up. Christ that was a lucky shot. You could barely see this little white patch. Henry, he knew about this bet I had going on with Makinson, and he piped up and said, "Well, I got twenty-five bucks on Bill." The other guys all started putting bets down on me too.

We still weren't sure if that white spot was a rabbit or not. We walked up a bit more and then I started to climb this cliff underneath the white spot. It was damn dangerous because the spring melt was just hitting and fracturing all the rocks. You'd grab at an outcropping and a lot of the time it'd just tumble down the cliff. I was up forty or fifty feet and found a couple of hawks nesting. They scared the hell out of me. I thought for sure they were going to hit me. They'd come diving in at me. I was stuck on the cliff, couldn't turn around or nothing, and I'd feel a little brush of air from these hawks swooping down on me. Finally I came down because I was scared they were going to hit me and knock me off. We never did find out what that white spot was, and Makinson, the bastard, never did show up for our match.

Makinson was always crazy about prospecting. Everywhere you went he'd bend over into all the little creeks looking for gold. The bugger figured he'd strike it rich up there. I knew this, and I had some gold nuggets that I always kept with me. I put them in a bottle and put a label on the bottom that said, "Discovered at Ookpik Creek, August 17th."

He come up one day and predictably started talking about big mineral strikes. When he was finished I hauled out this little bottle and I said, "I made a strike up there in the Ookpik. Found a bunch of nuggets." He asked to look at them and I said, "Oh, I was just bullshitting you. I got some samples but they're not gold, they're just copper." So I give him this bottle and he shakes out about half a dozen pea-sized nuggets. He started to tremble and said, "That's gold." I said, "No it isn't. Don't bullshit me. There's too goddamn much of it there to be gold." He insisted that it was gold. I said, "Couldn't be. I was up hunting caribou about a hundred miles inland and stopped for a drink in this creek. I lay down beside the creek and the goddamn gravel was full of this stuff. There was lots of it showing all over."

He wanted us to go up there right away and stake the creek. I said, "I'm not going all the way up there just to stake out some copper." Then he started bugging me to find out where the creek was. "I'm not going to tell you," I said. He said someone was going to find the creek and beat us to the gold, but I said, "No, I'm going out next year and I'll have the sample assayed. If it's gold, I'm chartering a plane up here to stake out this bloody creek."

He told the whole crew about how stupid I was. He said, "Crazy bugger doesn't know gold when he sees it. Bloody nuggets the size of peas." I went down to the *Roch* and they were all ragging on me about this until I filled them in. Jesus, they thought that was funny. We kept the charade up with Makinson for a while—kept asking him when he was going to set out and look for this Ookpik Creek.

I got Makinson a few times. He used to get seasick real easy. When we finally left Tree River at the end of July, I took a regular watch at the wheel. I'd wait until I seen him heading down to

Two unidentified Inuit men with Kells, Larsen and Makinson in Tree River, waiting for the ice to break up.

the galley to eat and I'd just lay the boat right into the trough so the old *Roch* would start rolling like a son of a bitch. He'd always come up and make straight for the rail. The crew all knew damn fine that I was doing it. Dad Parry would always get mad as hell about it. He'd yell, "Dirty work at the wheel, dirty work at the wheel."

A judge by the name of Douglas was already in Coppermine when we got there, along with a couple lawyers and a reporter from the *Chicago Tribune*. A real doll of a blonde, she was. She'd come in to cover the trial. They had a hell of a time rounding up a jury. Everyone had better things to do than watch a bunch of whites rag on some poor Inuit fellow. We rounded up all the loose traders in town, all six of them, and forced them to make up a jury. None of them wanted to apply the white man's laws to an Inuit, you see. Most of them all knew the Inuit well and figured they had better ways to deal with law and order than we did.

On the stand Ahigiak just repeated the story he'd told me. All the witnesses agreed with him and they also all agreed that Ahigiak had to stop his wife from being taken away somehow. The jury deliberated for fifteen minutes at the most and brought in a guilty verdict of manslaughter. Judge Douglas sentenced him to five years imprisonment in Aklavik. That was a joke. It meant he had to labour at the Aklavik police post for five years. He'd be able to draw on police rations and sit around the post just like the rest of the constables—basically his punishment was five years vacation with pay. He got to bring his wife too. You couldn't blame the Inuit for being confused about the workings of our justice system.

Douglas wasn't such a bad shit and had quite an interest in the north, thought of himself as quite an authority. He'd read Stefansson's books and was a real admirer of Stefansson, so one time him and I were out walking around the village and run into old Pannigabluk and I stopped to talk. He was quite impressed by her and says to me after she goes, "Who was that?"

"That was Mrs. Stefansson," I said.

"You mean…no!"

"Yeah, Pannigabluk," I said. "Stefansson's Inuit wife."

"Of course I know about Pannigabluk. Stefansson wrote about her at length. She was the expedition seamstress."

"Yeah, but that's not all she was," I said.

"How can you be so sure?" he said.

"Well, maybe we'll run into her son Alex Stefansson and he can tell you who his father is," I said. Douglas just shook his head. He couldn't believe the great Stefansson would have had an Inuit family and kept it secret, but it was true. Him and Pannigabluk were married northern style and had this one kid, Alex, but at the end of the expedition he just paid her off and never let on to the world. This was standard procedure among the old-timers, but Stefansson was such a champion of the Inuit the old judge was surprised to find out he was no better than the rest of them.

That fancy-looking reporter didn't do a single interview with me, but I saw her story a few years later. She started off with the usual old malarkey about the Mountie always getting his man and then she went on describing this big trip I went on to solve the murder. Then she added in a wild string of events that had no basis in fact whatsoever. Aside from all the travelling, that was about the easiest case there ever was to solve, but she made it sound like the Gunfight at the OK Corral with me standing in as Wyatt Earp. Other papers picked up on it, and the first thing I know friends and relatives are reading this malarkey all over down south. Later when I came out there were still reporters wanting to do a story about my big manhunt. It all added to the myth of RCMP heroics in the North, which is a goddamn joke.

24

HEADING BACK HOME

With the Ahigiak trial over, Ottawa decided the *Roch* should sail back to Vancouver. It was about bloody time. She was supposed to patrol up there for two years before going back down south, but she ended up staying there for four straight years. All that ramming into ice and sticking her up on rocks took a toll on the old girl and she needed a good refit.

I was getting to the end of my second term. Our postings lasted two years and I'd already had one extension. I loved the North, but I was nearly thirty years old and it seemed like time to get on with life. I figured I'd go back out on the *Roch* to Vancouver. I felt bad not saying goodbye to Mahik and Learmonth and all the rest in Cambridge—Christ, those guys were some of the best friends I ever had—but I had to make my move then and there or wait for another two years.

We made the usual few stops for fuel and supplies on the way down. I got Henry with a good prank when we were in port at Herschel. We always made sure to get tickets for the Irish Sweepstakes, you see. In those days lotteries were illegal in Canada, so the Irish was the only thing you could get. We'd

Bill back in a sailing outfit on the return trip to Vancouver.

have an outside agent buy the things for us and then he'd wire us the ticket numbers. The actual tickets came in the mail a few months later. One night I had quite a discussion with Henry about what a guy's chances actually were of winning the thing. He was more optimistic than I was. So I went up to Davies in the wireless cabin and we found the old wire giving Henry his ticket number. We put together a fake wire saying "Congratulations. Ticket number so-and-so has drawn first choice. More details to follow." And we made sure it was signed "Irish Sweepstakes Committee."

I went back down to the saloon and Davies followed a few minutes later with a telegram for Henry. He handed this envelope to Henry and said, "Congratulations, Henry." Henry opened the wire and said, "Jesus Christ. I've hit it." The rest of the crew crowded all around and read this telegram and we all started slapping his back. I asked him what he planned to do with all the money. He said, "I'm going to get a yacht and sail around the world." He figured the wire had to be authentic because it matched the ticket he had locked away in a drawer. Well, he had a talk with Davies the next day and that Davies just couldn't keep a straight face. Henry figured the hoax out pretty quickly. He was a hell of a good sport about it and laughed as much as anyone else.

Old Henry's girlfriend was the only one at the dock to meet us when we came into Vancouver. The two of them went up to his cabin to gather up some of his things. Everyone wanted to get off that boat as soon as possible because we knew that when Henry came back out of his cabin, he'd make someone stay behind and watch the boat while he went out for the night with his girlfriend. They were in his cabin about fifteen minutes and when he came out he had the whole boat to himself. We'd all buggered off before he could get in the way and stop us. Oh he was mad as hell too. He took a couple of days to catch up with us. They had to send guys down from a barge terminal to look after the boat.

First thing the rest of us did was go to a clothing store called Dick's. It was quarter to six and they closed at six o'clock, so they locked the doors behind us and let the five or six of us have the store to ourselves. Dick said that was the best day he ever had. He sold fifteen hundred dollars worth of duds inside half an hour.

The one thing Dick didn't sell was shoes. Everyone was still wearing their boat boots. Jack McCrae, the guy I nabbed crazy John Brown with, had come down with us. He was in such a hurry to leave the *Roch* he just threw on a pair of mukluks and he was walking all over town in these goddamn things. I was going someplace with McCrae, who I served watch with on the way down. We were walking down the street and we'd had a couple stiff ones by then. Mac was cussing these damn mukluks, so he said, "To hell with this." He stopped there on the curb and he took the mukluks off and left them there, started walking down the street in his sock feet. He kept watching everyone we walked by. Finally he saw this one guy with nice ankle boots that looked to be the right size, so he stopped this guy and said, "What do you want for your boots?" The guy didn't know. Mac said, "I'll give you twenty bucks for them." That's like a couple of hundred today. The guy couldn't get out of them quick enough. This was what McCrae wore that night.

I remember taking a cab to the Belmont Hotel. When I hopped in and it took off, I yelled to the driver, "Hey, take it easy. What's the rush?" We were just moving along at normal speed I guess, but life in the Arctic moves along at a pretty relaxed clip and I'd get awful anxious any time that cab went above twenty miles an hour.

The taxi driver brought all my clothes up to my hotel room and I gave him fifty bucks and told him to go get us some liquor. Fifty bucks would buy a lot of liquor in those days. So he come back up there and he had the damndest bunch of liquor and a big tub full of ice and beer. We didn't know how we were going to get rid of all the stuff. I didn't know anybody in Vancouver and there was only four of us left from off the boat. Some of the other guys had friends in Vancouver, so we called them up to give us a hand with all this booze, and several of them showed up. Two of them were up in my room and we were drinking. I wanted to head out on the town, so I got my glad rags on and went out circulating. I left the guys there. I don't know what time I got back, quite late. I come up, open the door to my room and they were just like a bunch of beached porpoises in there. There was maybe fifteen guys passed out—draped over the chairs and spread out on the carpet and such. What happened was, when

Bill fresh off the boat in Vancouver and looking dapper after an expensive visit to Dick's clothing store.

I'd left, these two guys drinking in my room got on the blower and said, "There's corn in Egypt, come on down." And so friends came. I never woke them up. I just left them there, got another room and never told them where it was.

When we came out we found the whole damn country was on the skids. We were pretty protected as long as we stayed in the North. Fox prices went from over sixty bucks a pelt the year I went up down to around seventeen when I left. That was the only sign of the doggone Depression I ever seen in the Arctic. But I knew a little about what was happening outside because my brothers kept in touch by mail. Dad had actually lost the farm in those years, but it was hard to get a picture of how wide-spread the troubles were. Boy, what a scene in Vancouver. So many people just looking absolutely destitute.

The government took the same attitude as most of the constables I met. They were all right wing as hell and figured a man without work was just an idler, even in the depths of the Great Depression with a third of the workforce out on the streets. And I think old Flashlight Akins must've seen a few promotions, because there was a real red scare on. All the brass were saying "watch out for the commies." In the spring of 1935 a bunch of unemployed guys organized the On-to-Ottawa Trek. They were planning to ride the rails all the way to Ottawa and give the prime minister hell. They figured on holding quite a rally out in Regina and the brass wanted me to head out there. Well, I joined the Mounties to see the North, not to go around beating up unemployed Depression victims, so I quit. Even with ten thousand bucks in my pocket, what with a couple years travelling around and everybody I knew on the bum, it wasn't long before I was just as hard up as the rest of them.

25

THE IN-BETWEEN YEARS

I always had it in the back of my mind that I'd get back to the North someday, but I got sidetracked for forty years. I did get back as close as Dawson City, where I went diamond drilling for old General Odlum, but then I got married. I'd met Ivy when I first came down from the Arctic, and when I came back from the Yukon she was going to meet my boat but I got waylaid and she ended up meeting empty boats for a week or so. By the time I finally got in she'd gave up, so I had to go up to Woodward's store where she was working and look her up. I guess she'd been doing quite a propaganda job on the other salesgirls because I remember getting looked over pretty careful. I'm afraid I didn't measure up too good because it just turned out I was wearing a hell of a big purple-and-yellow shiner. I'd got tangling arseholes with some bastard before I left Dawson and zigged when I should have zagged. Ivy, I guess, was pretty embarrassed, but she got used to that.

That's funny when you think about it because we couldn't help becoming heroes up north, even when all we did most of the time was sit around the post and play crib. After I got married I went into union work, where I was really busting my ass

Bill with Ivy and their first child, Marilyn, early in 1942.

to make things better for the average joe, and that's when I found out I was a public enemy. This was during the great wartime shipping boom, and I got to be head of the Marine Workers and Boilermakers Union, which at that time was the largest local union in Canada. The newspapers took a new view of me then and from that time on I couldn't do anything but I come out looking like a villain.

Still, I wouldn't have missed it. It was a big job and I got to do a lot of things I never would have otherwise, except maybe get put in jail. I pulled a shift in Oakalla there one time for refusing to obey a phony court order. On the plus side, I got to go to London to defend the rights of unions before the British Privy Council. It was the last case heard by the Privy Council before Canada went on its own, and we won it, too. *Kuzych vs. White* it's referred to as, and it became a legal landmark throughout the Commonwealth. So I've got my name in the books there someplace anyways. It kind of looks like that'll be the only place, too. But that suits me fine. I would just as soon have my name on an important labour case as a bridge or a highway like some of the phonies I used to tangle with.

I was re-elected president of the Marine Workers eleven straight times before I finally resigned in 1955. Those years just went by in a blur. You never had time to look to the left or the right, your both hands were tied up dealing with all the things that kept coming up in front of you. I didn't have enough family life to mention. Our daughters, Marilyn and Shirley, were grown up almost before I knew it. As Ivy was very fond of saying, I was married to the union.

I was fifty by the time I left the union, and after running a mill up in the Cariboo for a few years and doing some construction, I built a house on a piece of waterfront I'd picked up in Pender Harbour, where I spend a little time developing the property and a lot of time fishing.

They say once you've seen the midnight sun the North is in your

Bill as head of the Marine Workers and Boilermakers Union.

blood, and I guess that's true enough in my case. I always paid special attention to anything I heard about it in the news and I kept in touch with some of the guys.

Old Rudolph Johnson was one of our favourites. Ivy liked him and we'd have him over to the house whenever we could. He was a great character. One year he came out with a twenty-thousand-dollar stake in the fall and blew it all by spring. He had expert help, though—he hooked up with a dame in Vancouver they called the Danish Queen who had a lot of experience at helping guys blow their stakes. She'd been over the road before they rolled the rocks off, that one. One thing about it, it made me feel a lot better about taking a couple years to blow a stake half that size. Rudolph didn't give a damn. He was great company and through him I'd keep up on gossip about the North.

Learmonth was another one. He stayed in the Arctic for forty-six years and finally retired to Ontario. We'd exchange letters, and a couple times I went out to visit. His house was absolutely full of Arctic relics. He had the greatest collection of books about the North I ever saw and he was a walking encyclopedia himself. He was a recognized authority, and different museums hired him to do archaeology and collecting while he was still in the North. I told him he should write a book, and he could have done a great one too, but he wouldn't even consider it. He was too humble. The only thing he would write was the odd piece in the Hudson's Bay Company magazine *The Beaver*, mostly to set other guys straight on their facts. To him the north was kind of sacred, and he just hated all these people like Duncan Pryde who churned out bullshit about it and went around grandstanding. He really had it in for Henry toward the end because of that. They'd been friends, and he figured Henry should have known better.

It's a damn funny thing, but Henry became the star of that whole show. Henry, of all people. Here's this real ordinary guy who wasn't a trained cop and worked quietly away as the RCMP boatman for twenty years, but in the end he became more famous than Steele or Dempster or Fitzgerald or any of the RCMP's big names up north. They named a stretch of water up there after him, put his name on a government icebreaker and built a special museum in Vancouver for the *Roch*.

A lot of this was to do with a stunt they pulled during the war. The government wanted to put on a show to beef up Canada's hold over the north, so they ordered Henry to take the *Roch* into the eastern arctic, figuring to blow a bunch of smoke about conquering the Northwest Passage. This was a bit of a joke because the so-called Northwest Passage was a busy bloody highway by this time with trading posts all along it and supply ships like the

Chimo and the *Aklavik* going this way and that way every year. Not too many crossed through from west to east, but I know the *Aklavik* did in 1938 and Henry knew it too. He tried the same route in 1941 but run into bad ice and got froze up west of the Boothia Peninsula.

He had been supposed to meet a Hudson's Bay supply ship called the *Nascopie* coming east at Fort Ross. The *Nascopie* had nine dogs from Greenland that were supposed to go aboard the *Roch*. Henry was pretty desperate to get these dogs because they had no way of getting around on the ice without them. He radioed Fort Ross saying he wanted the dogs brought over as soon as the ice was thick enough. He said he was in Cape Christian, just three days from Ross. Well, a couple Inuit head out from Ross to Cape Christian to drop off the dogs, and they roam around for ten days, but they don't see any bloody ship there and they head back to Fort Ross. They get back on the radio with Henry and ask him if he's sure he's in Cape Christian. Turns out he's not so sure. They finally figured out that he was in Pasley Bay, a hundred miles from Cape Christian. A bit embarrassing for a guy making his name as one of the country's great navigators.

They didn't get loose until the next August and after battling a lot of bad ice finally made it to Halifax in October. They spent a year on patrol in the Eastern Arctic, then in 1944 went back to the west taking the northern route around Baffin Island and through Viscount Melville Sound. They had better ice conditions this time and made the trip in eighty-six days from Halifax to Vancouver. My old friend Rudolph Johnson shipped as second engineer on this trip and he said it was like a summer cruise.

A lot of people think the *Roch* conquered the Northwest Passage, but Amundsen's *Gjoa* did that in 1905. The *Roch* is supposed to be first to do it from west to east and do it both ways, but the *Aklavik* crossed the main part both ways in 1938. It might be true the Roch was the first to take the top route and circle America in two jumps, but it gets a bit strained. Just the same, they ballyhooed it to the skies and promoted Henry to superintendent in charge of the whole Arctic.

According to Learmonth, the attention Henry got went to his head and turned him into a different guy from the one we'd both known. He told me a story that showed how much Henry got caught up in the polar fame game.

The US Army was staging a big manoeuvre up around Cambridge Bay—this must've been the late '40s. They planned to bring a big contingent from Baker Lake up to Cambridge, then down through Coppermine and back to Baker Lake, travelling on snow cats. Henry was wintering in Cambridge on the *Roch,* and when he heard that they were going to come across from Perry River to Cambridge he decided he'd go out and meet them and guide them in. He struck off alone by dogsled. He got out to Cape Callborn, about twelve miles out of Cambridge, and he ran into rough ice. While he was trying to figure out how to get through it, these army fellows just went out around him. They didn't need any guidance at all. They had planes and everything. They just went around the rough ice on these snowcats doing twenty, thirty miles an hour and got into Cambridge a day before Henry.

The army group changed plans and decided to go up the east coast of Victoria Island, so Henry figured he'd guide them there. He struck off a couple days ahead and got up there about thirty miles or so when the snowcats passed him. These cats roared up to the top of Victoria Island, turned around, come back and passed Henry again while he was still on his way up. Learmonth said everyone knew what Henry was up to. There was lots of press following this expedition and he wanted to be seen as this grand old Arctic explorer showing the new guys the way, but it turned into a complete fiasco.

They finally retired the *Roch* in 1948 and Henry passed on in 1964. In '66 they had a big do for the *Roch* because they'd put together the money to house her permanently in the Vancouver Maritime Museum. Henry's widow was there and a few of the original crew all got to sit up on a big stage while the mayor, the Minister of Northern Affairs and a few RCMP brass made speeches. I don't think anybody even knew I was there. Of course they laid it on real heavy about the conquest of the Northwest Passage as if that was the only thing Henry and the *Roch* ever did. They had another big do in 1987 when they launched the big icebreaker *Henry Larsen*, and this time they hauled me up on the stage with the big-wigs. I was long retired of course but it was my old union who'd built the thing, so the new president made a hell of a ruckus about that. He said, "We have here today a man who not only served with Henry Larsen aboard the *St. Roch*, but is also a past-president of the shipbuilder's union."

I wish Henry could have been there to see this ship. It's supposed to go through eight foot of ice and has more than ten thousand horsepower. I asked the captain how they protected the propellers, because that used to be a big thing with the Arctic ships. "We don't bother with that," he said. "We just back right into the ice and the prop grinds it up like hamburger." Henry wouldn't have believed that.

I like to think of Henry the way I knew him and not as the stuffed shirt they made him into. When I knew him he was a good joe—just one of the gang. He was a good ice pilot and his real achievement was surviving twenty seasons in the North without losing the ship—though he came close a few times.

Christ, he and I went on quite a bender the last time I ever saw him, in 1937. Me, Henry and that big dog of his spent a whole night going around to every bootleg joint in Vancouver.

I gave Henry that dog. I raised quite a few dogs up north and I raised this one to be a lead dog. He was a good one too, but he turned into a killer. He'd started going after the other dogs. I was going to shoot him, but Henry came along and said he'd try and train this dog out of it. He done a good job, but he told me about one time this dog got him into a real pickle.

Henry was living in Victoria at the time and these two old maids living next door had a ginger tomcat they pampered something terrible. This one day Henry was sitting on his porch and they were sitting on their porch, yakking back and forth between the two yards, when this tomcat comes strolling into Henry's yard through a hole in the fence. Henry's dog spotted this cat and pricked up his ears a little. The cat furred up a bit but just kept ambling through the yard like he owned the place. Henry didn't think nothing of it.

That dog let the cat get within fifteen feet, then rushed it and flipped it right up in the air with a broken back. These women started shrieking and all Henry can think to do is stop the cat from suffering, so he grabs it by the tail and swings its head against the dirt so as to bash out its brains and the women start shrieking even louder. Jesus, did old Henry ever feel bad about that. As he was telling me the story he got kind of choked up— almost bawling remembering how he had killed the old ladies' cat. He had a soft heart and really loved people and animals. That's the way I like to remember him.

26

RETURN TRIP

I finally made it back to Cambridge Bay in 1974. I wanted to see if there was any old Inuit I still knew so bought an airline ticket and headed up.

Coming into Cambridge from the air was a whole new thing. The place had grown. There were maybe a hundred permanent shacks spread out where there couldn't have been more than ten in the '30s. A guy by the name of Billy Lyall met me when I come off the plane. He was a real live wire and a champion of Inuit rights who helped get a co-operative in Cambridge up and running. I got in touch with him before I went up and he found a place for me to stay. They called it the Royal Hilton and it was a plywood bunkhouse about forty feet long with a dozen or so steel bunks.

On the way to the Royal Hilton I started asking Lyall about Cambridge. He told me that somewhere around ninety percent of the residents were on welfare and they were mostly living in little matchbox houses with the windows all boarded up. Seven or eight hundred people lived there year-round. Well there's no way Cambridge Bay can support that many people. It was always a poor place for hunting. That's why every family lived at least twenty miles from one another back in the thirties. Staying in one spot all year and relying on government handouts changed the Inuit from what I used to know. During my years in the North as a Mountie, I never once saw a drunk Inuit. Now they had nothing better to do. Black eyes and cuts and bruises were pretty common sights.

There were hardly any dogs, damn few hunted and nobody but a few Inuit elders knew the history of the place. My second day, the principal of the school—I guess he heard about my Mountie days—he come up to me and asks if I'd go speak to the school. I said, "Sure, that sounds fine."

I got into this little schoolhouse they had there and I guess seventy-five percent of the kids were Inuit and the rest of them were white. What a sad state of affairs. Here's a washed-up old Mountie who hasn't been in the Arctic for forty-three years teaching these kids about their own doggone country. That's just how far things had gone. I told them about all kinds of stuff: how we used to hunt for seal, how we built snowhouses, how we used to make mail runs, and as far as I could tell it was all new to them.

You see, things were already starting on the downhill path when I was up there the first time. Around 1924, the first trading posts came to Victoria Land and King William Land. There'd been contact with whites before that, but not enough to change much. But when these posts come along they started convincing the natives to trap white fox. In return for foxes the natives got rifles and metal pots and matchsticks and whatever else they wanted. The natives around that area never trapped before that, they were hunters. Goddamn, were they ever exploited. A good trade in those days was one fox for six biscuits or one fox for a package of needles. These types of things cost you less than a dime anywhere else. When I first went in there it was thirty foxes for a rifle, three foxes for package of ammunition, a fox for a spool of thread, a fox for a brass lighter—just terrible.

So this was how the Inuit got hold of rifles. They just had

arrows and spears before that. Now with these rifles, they shot caribou by the dozen—the skins were worth a good deal more than fox pelts at the trading posts. And the posts gave out free traps, so the traplines got longer and longer and the Inuit need-ed more dogs and more food and more ammunition. Weren't all that many dogs up there before the posts came along. The Inuit just used to use the dogs to find seal holes, but here they were having to hitch more than half a dozen to a sled just to make a living. It wasn't long before the whole thing spiralled right out of bloody control. The caribou populations crashed some time in the fifties. But they were already getting scarce when I was up there in the thirties.

I found out that Angulalik and Mahik were both still alive and circulating around Cambridge. I went to see Mahik first. He was always the one I was closest to. He came with me on just about every trip I ever made up there. I found out where he lived and went over to his house. There were about eight or nine Inuit in there, most of them young guys. So I strolled up to Mahik and asked in Inuktitut, "Have you ever seen me before?" He kind of scratched his head for a while and said he didn't recognize me. I said, "I shoved you down a seal hole many years ago." That did it. He jumped right up and gave me a big hug and slapped me on the back. Then he turned around and told all the young guys I was the Mountie he travelled around with back in the old days and he told them the story of me shoving him down a seal hole.

It was a real happy visit until we sat down and Mahik started filling me in on all that'd gone on in the last forty years. His wife Hukonga passed on a number of years before and he married another women by the name of Elimatuk, but she died too. Now he was on the prowl for wife number three, but he wasn't too interested in any of the young ones. He said, "They all drink too much and none of them can sew my boots."

"You don't need a wife now," I said. "It used to be our peck-ers were big and our bellies were small, now we're old men and our peckers are small and our bellies are big. We got no use for wives anymore." He laughed to beat hell and repeated that to everyone he saw.

We talked about some of the old traders and some of the cops. He said most of those guys who headed up there were "tickyhoks"—greenhorns. They were more office men than anything. Very few of them knew how to speak Inuktitut. Henry knew a few words. Anderton knew a few words too, but neither of them were fluent.

He told me that the less people hunted the more they got into the booze. Sam Carter, the guide I had when I was doing the census, and his wife Owpulluktuk had died from drinking. Mahik said that not long after I left, Angulalik had gone on trial for murder. Now I don't know who'd fight with Angulalik—he was just a little wee squirt not more than five feet high and a hundred pounds—but Mahik told me some big fellow started to roughhouse Angulalik. They'd had two or three run-ins before. During the last one Angulalik pulled a jackknife out, and this guy grabbed him, but Angulalik sliced him right up the belly with the knife so that all his guts spilled out. This guy tried to run outside and he tripped over his own guts. They say he might've lived if he hadn't have pulled all his guts out from walking on them. The Mounties took Angulalik in and tried him for murder down at Coppermine. He got off and there was a big celebration. Everybody went on a big drunk. Sam and Owpulluktuk drank methyl hydrate that night and died. In all, there was only about six Inuit still living in Cambridge that I remembered.

The hunting wasn't much good anymore but Mahik's stepson, David Kaomayok, was the best around. In the spring of that year a group of Inuit had gone out hunting for polar bear and come back skunked. Then this Kaomayok went out and he come back with five of the big bastards. He had artificial legs, that guy. Both his legs were amputated from the knee down. He got quite a laugh when I asked him if he ever got cold feet.

There was still some relics of my time there. Back in the

Bill with Angulalik on his trip to Cambridge in 1974.

Bill with Mahik on the same trip.

thirties I built an icehouse in one of the hills. I'd shovelled down for a few feet until I hit permafrost and then grabbed a couple old hatch covers off the *Maud* and used them to cover up the hole. I insulated the whole thing with layers of snow and old coal sacks. Jesus that thing worked good. We used to throw all our fish and meat in there and it'd keep all year long. I went to have a look at the thing in '74 just to see if it was still there, but it'd been ripped up. The constables there told me that a couple years before some kids went and vandalized the thing. But the old detachment that Wilson and I built in '32 was still in use.

The second night up there, Billy Lyall said to me that a bunch of them were going to go fishing up at Ikluktutiak Lake. He had a snowmobile and pulled me behind it in a sled. It was around June I went up there, so things were melting and there were pools of water everywhere. Jesus, that goddamn water would splash all over me. He gave me a fishing line, just a jig

Bill with a fishing party in 1974. Bill was the only one among them to catch anything.

line. I went and found a crack in the ice. It was still good and thick but it was starting to crack in places. I started to fish, and there was about sixteen or eighteen natives there that night. There was two fish caught that night and I caught both of them. They all laughed, said the old man had gone and come back after forty years to teach them all to fish. It was just luck. There was a Frenchman up there that night and he couldn't get over it. He came over and said, "How the hell you do that? What's the trick?"

On the way back in that sled I got soaking wet. It was below zero, so by the time we got to Cambridge I was just like a big ice cake.

I pretty near got into a rhubarb up there. The school had burned down and there was a bunch of white construction workers rebuilding it. They were staying right beside me in the Royal Hilton. Holy Jesus, did I get so goddamn mad at them.

They'd be swearing about the Inuit, "These black bastards. You give them a good job and they don't give a shit. They're just lazy. If they don't feel like working they just fuck off and go fishing or something."

I heard them saying this and just tied into the bastards. We really got hot and heavy. I said, "Look, they didn't ask you bastards to come here. They got along just fine before white men came. They've lived here for thousands of years." But that didn't faze them, you know. They just figured I was some old tourist in for a vacation and didn't take me seriously.

The final straw was when a little native guy come in with some little soapstone carvings of geese—"niglik" they call them. He couldn't speak English and he was showing the rednecks these geese and they said, "What the hell do you want? Why don't you speak proper." They just treated him like shit, you know. So I went up to this guy and struck up a conversation in Inuktitut. He was selling these little carvings. I said, "How much?" He said, "Five bucks." I give him five bucks and got three little carvings. These rednecks nearly fell off their goddamn chairs. "Holy Christ," they said, "where did you learn the language like that?" I said, "Oh, forty years ago when I lived with the black bastards. I sure as hell prefer them to you ignorant buggers," and I walked outside to stay at Mahik's place. There's only so much ignorance a guy can put up with in one lifetime.

AFTERWORD

Not long after he settled back into the comfort of his waterfront home in Pender Harbour, BC, Bill was saddened by the news that Mahik had died in an accident. Bill's old seal-hunting partner had taken his decrepit snowmobile out on a fishing trip and hit a thin spot in the ice. The machine broke through, taking Mahik with it.

Bill hadn't formed any particular plans to visit Mahik again, but the fact he would never be able to hit him hard. As his own life wound down, he often reflected that his years in the Arctic were "the best years of my life." So, when family members approached him during his final months with the idea of having his ashes spread at Cambridge Bay, he gave his enthusiastic blessing. When he died on July 20, 2001, his ashes were soon flown to Yellowknife. Poor weather delayed the last leg of his journey to Cambridge until the chilly days of October.

On a windy autumn day, snow crunching underfoot, two active Mounties, a priest and two Inuit elders stood on Mount Pelly, the hill overlooking Cambridge Bay, with Bill's ashes. His previous visit to the hill had been on a miserable spring day in 1932. Sydney Cornwall, former captain of the *Bay Chimo*, was held over in Cambridge by snow and wind. An inveterate gambler, Cornwall bet Bill that it wasn't possible in the blustery, frigid conditions to hike up and down Mount Pelly between sunrise and sunset, a window of only a few hours. Bill, no stranger to a bet himself, strapped on his snowshoes and bounded up Mount Pelly. At the top, he pushed a stick into the snow and tied a piece of red cloth to it as proof of his ascent. He arrived back at the post with the sun still hanging low over the mountains. An impressed Cornwall paid up.

Seventy years later, on Bill's final trip up Pelly, the sun was again hanging low over the horizon, casting a golden glow across the almost featureless landscape that had taken such a hold upon him. The two elders, eighty-five-year-old Luke Novoligak, who remembered Bill White, and Moses Koihok, said a few words in the language Bill had taken such pride in sharing with them. The priest, Russ Blanchett, said a few more in English before Constable Dean Larkin spread the ashes.

Mount Pelly is the highest point for miles around Cambridge Bay. The view at the top is a 360-degree panorama, a majestic setting for sunrises and sunsets. But in the dark months, and even in the bright ones, eyes will always turn towards the bay below and the village huddled around it. Today, with 1,300 residents, it sprawls beyond the boundaries Bill remembered. But it still belongs to the Arctic, where life is still constrained by extreme nature and where old relics crumble slowly. There remains the hulk of a ship, minus a forty-foot boom and the alcohol from its compass, resting on the bay's bottom. There remains a small wooden shack, hammered together in the spring of 1932 to serve as a police post, now housing a freshly painted RCMP museum. And atop Mount Pelly, Bill White is back among the people he unreservedly admired in the land he could never completely leave.

Acknowledgements

I have been fortunate in having the support and assistance of many people in the writing of this book. From the beginning, the staff of the Vancouver Maritime Museum has been very generous with their assistance in research and photographs. Bill White's daughter Marilyn Bueckert has been a great encourager and contributed in many ways, not the least being the many hours she and her partner Richard spent rounding up and identifying family photographs. Senator Pat Carney was most obliging in reading the text and leading me to the Nunavut Archives where Edward Atkinson and Lazarie Otak gave invaluable help with Inuit names and spellings. For access to tapes and notes of their conversations with Bill White made over the years between 1971 and 2000, I am indebted to my grandfather Frank White and my father, Howard White, whose unwavering support made this project possible. To the staff of Harbour Publishing, including Peter Read for his fine cover design, Patricia Wolfe for her keen-eyed editing, Roger Handling for his mapping, Mary White for her interior layout, Alicia Miller and Marisa Alps for the unsung heroics of the marketing department and Vici Johnstone for everything else, my grateful thanks. To Edith Iglauer I am eternally indebted, not just for her flattering preface, but for her unstinting encouragement and her inspirational example to all who dare to follow in her trailblazing footsteps. Sarah, thank you for your subversive help and for your patience. And finally Mum, thank you for being such an inexhaustible source of encouragement, grammatical advice, good cooking—and for being such an infallible bullshit detector—this past year and all previous. This book is for you.

Bibliography

Unpublished Sources

White, Franklin Howard, unpublished journals 1970–2001
White, Lundy William Lloyd and White, Franklin Wetmore, taped interviews 1997–2000
White, Lundy William Lloyd, "Like It Was," 1974, unpublished manuscript.
White, Lundy William Lloyd, and White, Franklin Howard, taped interviews 1970–1996
White, Lundy William Lloyd, personal papers kept by Marilyn Bueckert; arctic photograph album 1930–1935
Vancouver Maritime Museum, *St. Roch* archive files.

Published Sources

Campbell, William, *Arctic Patrols: Stories of the Royal Canadian Mounted Police* (Bruce, 1936).
Delgado, James P. *Arctic Workhorse: The RCMP Schooner* St. Roch (Touchwood, 2003).
De Poncins, Gontran and Galantiere, Lewis, *Kabloona* (Reynal and Hitchcock, 1941).
Dobrowolsky, Helene, *Law of the Yukon* (Lost Moose Publishers, 1995).
Farrar, Frederick, *Arctic Assignment*, (MacMillan, 1963).
Francis, Daniel, *Arctic Chase: A History of Whaling in Canada's North* (Breakwater Books, 1984).
———, *Discovery of the North: The Exploration of Canada's Arctic* (Hurtig Publishers, 1986).
Freuchen, Peter, *Book of the Eskimos* (Fawcett Crest, 1965).
Greene, Ruth, *Personality Ships of British Columbia* (Marine Tapestry Publications, 1969).

Iglauer, Edith, *Inuit Journey* (Harbour Publishing, 2000).

Kelly, William and Nora, *The Royal Canadian Mounted Police, A Centennial History* (Hurtig Publishers, 1973).

Larsen, Henry A. with Sheer, Frank R. and Omholt-Jensen, Edvard, *The Big Ship* (McClelland and Stewart, 1967).

LeBourdais, D.M., *Stefansson: Ambassador of the North* (Harvest House, 1963).

Lyall, Ernie, *An Arctic Man* (Hurtig Publishers, 1979).

Royal Canadian Mounted Police, *Royal Canadian Mounted Police: An Historical Outline* ([RCMP] Headquarters, 1967).

Stefansson, Vilhjalmur, *My Life With the Eskimo* (The Macmillan Company, 1913).

————, *The Friendly Arctic* (The Macmillan Company, 1921).

————, *Unsolved Mysteries of the Arctic* (Collier Books, 1970).

Steele, Harwood Elmes Robert, *Policing the Arctic* (London: Jarrolds, 1936).

Stewart, Robert, *Sam Steele: Lion of the Frontier* (Toronto: Nelson, 1979).

White, Howard, *A Hard Man to Beat* (Pulp Press Book Publishers, 1983).

Index